NO BullShit Business Finance Guide

By

Bill King ASBC, CLFP, CLBB

Bill King
Published By: 4 Kings Capital Publishing,
A division of 4 Kings Capital LLC
469-277-7988
www.4KingsCapital.com
www.NoBullshitBusinessFinanceGuide.com

First Edition 2021
E Book ISBN 978-1-7369974-0-6
Paperback Edition ISBN 978-0-578-88928-3
Hardcover Edition ISBN 978-1-7369974-1-3

Foreword

I'd give this book to a friend. It's that good. I'm not saying that Bill is Ernest Hemingway, but he is damn funny, candid, and very good at explaining how you get financing. The challenge of the financing process is partially about knowing what the various products are and what the steps are to get a lender's money into your business bank account. Bill covers both of those topics in this book. However, the other challenges are as important to address: Setting realistic expectations and understanding what goes on behind that curtain at the Bank of Oz. Bill covers both of those challenges as well. If your expectations are unrealistic and if you don't know what goes on behind that curtain, the financing process is likely going to be a frustrating experience for you. So, if you want to avoid the expense of replacing your laptop, that you may hurl across the room out of frustration with lenders. And if you want to save your profanity for when your favorite sports team loses a game, then do yourself a favor and buy this book. Rip the curtain.
Saji George Business Development Officer Internex Capital

"As a banker, I prefer to work with someone like Bill at 4 Kings Capital. Bill makes my job easier when presenting financing requests for his clients. This is because of his extensive industry knowledge and his no-nonsense approach to helping his clients get access to the capital they need on the best terms possible."
Tracy Corley
SBA BDO
Fidelity Bank

In my time working with Bill, I see the passion he has for helping small business owners get the financing they need to launch or grow their businesses! He is undoubtedly knowledgeable, but beyond that, he really takes the time to understand his client's needs to give them the best guidance possible. I highly recommend this book to any business owner who needs help navigating the challenging world of business finance!

Dave Papenmeir

Life Coach

Your Next PERFECT Step

When you look up "business finance" in the dictionary, you'll see that the definition is "Bill King." Put another way, the name Bill King is synonymous with the term business finance. Bill's extensive knowledge in the business finance sector is a result of his multiple decades worth of experience in the space. When working with someone on any sort of business financing need, you want someone who has "been there, done that" and can advise and provide you with the best solution the market has to offer and clearly explain why it's the best route to go. Bill is that "someone." On top of that, Bill provides excellent customer service. He is responsive and friendly, and easy to talk to. He is the epitome of first class professionalism. Thank you, Bill, for always delivering!

Michael Ian Reeder – CPA

Are you seeking funding but don't know where to start? Small, medium, or large, even the startup will gain Bill's years of expertise and all the benefits from his incredible network of financial sources and options. Easy to work alongside of and one of the best business partners we have ever had.

Dr. Lorie J Clark – CFO

Vector Systems Inc

Bill is an expert when it comes to commercial finance. He understands how to navigate during volatile times in the economy. He brings excellent perception to the marketplace.

Stu Schlackman

Competitive Excellence

Acknowledgements

I'd like to thank all of my clients, referral partners, financing sources and other business friends that have helped our company thrive. I'd also like to thank all of the banks I've worked for over the years. My experiences (good and bad) and training have given me some great insights shared in this book.

Last and definitely not least, I'd like to thank the Queen, my lovely wife Veronica. For over 20 years, you have been my soft place to fall with all the trials we have gone through. Without your help, this book would have just been the ramblings of an old banker. Thank you, and I love you (no, she didn't write this part). There's a story near the end of the book where you guys will see a great example of just how strong she really is.

I'm sure there are other people that I missed, but I appreciate everyone who has been a part of this journey. Now, on with the book.

Table of Contents

Chapter 1

The Reality

"Drive thy Business, or it will drive thee." - Benjamin Franklin

The Hit and Fall

Defeat overwhelmed her as she heard him enter the front door. She knew that a quick meeting meant bad news. Arms ready to hold him was all she could offer her burdened husband. She took a deep breath as his footsteps headed toward the kitchen where she stood. His eyes glanced at the floor, then looked up to meet hers. "I did all I could, but our business can't be saved," he said, trying to sound strong.

They embraced right there in the middle of the kitchen with the smell of coffee still in the air. Neither said a word. The quiet hovered as if taunting that their dream might be coming to an end.

"What did they say?" She finally asked, breaking the silence.

"Same thing they always say, 'We're sorry, but we can't lend you any more money. Times are tough everywhere. Our bank isn't lending in that space right now'- whatever that means. It's always the same damn bullshit I keep hearing."

"I'm so sorry, honey," she said as her mind raced. "Did you tell them it's not that we aren't making sales but that we just need something to get us through these cycles?"

"Yes, yes! But they won't listen," he answered coming out of her embrace. "I can talk till I'm blue in the face, and the answer is still the same. Why can't they see what a good business we have? It's like they don't care how much we are growing. Everything we've done up to this point doesn't seem to matter to the bank."

He shook his head in disbelief, trying to fight back anger and hurt. "We have people that depend on us. How are we going to keep helping them? I'm just so tired of hearing no... Five years running this business, and it feels like we have nothing to show for it."

She grabbed his hand and kissed his cheek, motioning him to sit down. "Let me get you some coffee,'" she said, searching for a cup. Her eyes glanced over to him and recognized the disappointment and self-doubt on his face.

"Stop it," she said, handing him the hot mug.

"What?" he responded coyly, knowing there was nothing he could hide from her.

"You know 'what.' Don't you start beating yourself up. I won't have it."

"I don't mean to," he paused, lowering his head. "But honey, I feel like such a failure. I feel like I've let you, the kids, our employees- the whole damn world down. And now I'm probably going to have to close the doors on something we worked so hard to have."

She hugged him from behind, unable to stop the tears filling her eyes but refusing to let them fall. "Stop, just stop. You are not a failure; you hear me. You are the hardest working man I know. You built this from nothing. We just have to figure out another way to get the money to keep us going."

He closed his eyes. The darkness engulfed any light left in him. "Our dream is vanishing before me, and there is not a damn thing I can do about it. Maybe everyone was right. I should have just stuck to my nine to five job. Even if I hated it."

"You don't mean that. Besides, that man is not who you were meant to be," she said as the hot tears covered her face. "You and I both know it,"

"I know," he said, broken but trying hard to smile. "There just has to be **another way...**"

In the Reality there is Hope

Similar scenarios happen every day in the business world. Perhaps it may even be close to happening to you or someone you know. I am here to tell you that not all hope is lost.

Though most business owners and entrepreneurs are wonderful in their field, most are not taught the ins and outs of financing, revolving lines of credit, or even what makes them a desirable candidate for most banks. Capital is part of the foundation that is required to run those businesses. It is also a big factor that can be easily overlooked as companies start to grow.

Most people believe and even expect business owners to know everything about finance, but that is just an impossibility. It is a constantly changing force that can shift from one season to the next. Unless you work in the banking field, are an analyst, or even an auditor, there is no way you would know all there is to learn while still running the day to day demands of a business.

The sobering statistics are that roughly 50% of Small Businesses fail in the US in the first two years. Out of the remaining that do survive, only another 50% will last beyond five years. Polls showed that 80% of the unfortunately failed businesses attribute their demise to lack of cash flow. It is mind-boggling to think that Access to Capital is consistently ranked in the top three challenges faced by entrepreneurs every day. Our goal is to help make that a little easier and show you there is a way not to become part of those statistics.

Getting a loan, as most of you know, is a difficult process. It is also one that is not often talked about. Even though this battle plays a big part in the overall functioning of your company, it is an important part that you can get ahead of. So, before you lose hope and think, "Well, I'm screwed!" know there are ways around this. Help is out there.

What if there was a way to increase your chances of getting a loan approved faster and easier? The best way to do this is by taking you behind the scenes of the Big Bank, Small Bank lender, and other sources most people do not even know about. I guarantee they do not see the information you present the same way business owners do.

In this book, I will give you tools that will help your business "Self-evaluate" and understand whether you are bankable and what to do if you are not. With banking regulations, there are a great deal of restrictions put on how much information they can share as to WHY your loan was turned down.

I am here to help point you in the right direction. Now there are some tough deals out there, and I am the type of ex-banker turned consultant that WILL tell you if it is bankable. But I am also the type that will not bullshit you when I know there is no way in hell we can make it happen. Not all deals will work, but I can try to show you why and what you can do to make them stronger.

This is NOT a guarantee that all deals will get the funding they need. I am not Santa Claus and will not be able to give you the perfect gift. But this book can point you in the right direction of what needs to be done. This is what the couple in our kitchen scene needed. It is **Another Way.**

I wrote this book for privately held business owners of all types because I have deep respect for those that put so much on the line. Simply put, I wanted to help. Perhaps you have been in business for a few years, a decade or generations, but you could use extra capital to keep the day to day going. You may even be looking to expand. This book will guide you through that.

As I mentioned above, most business owners are great at what they do but are usually not familiar with the ins and outs of the financing process. I decided to lay it out in this book.

First, I dispel a few myths you hear in the market. Then I dive into the mind of a banker, outlining the 5 C's of credit. After that, cover some of the different financing situations you will find yourself in, such as needing working capital for operations, buying equipment, and investing in real estate.

I even take you behind the scenes at the bank and show what it really means when the lender says your deal "Is in Underwriting." One of my favorites is a behind curtain reveal of Six Dirty Words the banker said, but you may not have heard. Knowing this tip alone could save you a lot of process time.

Lastly, we walk you through the components of a good loan package and why certain items are important that most people may not have considered. Even answering questions like, "What happens if the bank says no?" We have you covered there as well with some information on alternative financing sources. So, buckle up, grab a cup of coffee, and dive in. Let us cut through the bullshit!

Chapter 2

Myths in Money Fairy Land

"There are three kinds of lies: lies, damn lies, and statistics." -
Benjamin Disraeli

Non-Recourse No Money Down Myths

I am about to piss off a lot of infomercial people and investment real estate syndicates with this myth. As I mentioned before, there are many people who make a living trying to sell us on the "easy button." I am sure you guys have all heard this one before- "No credit, bad credit, no problem! You do not have any money to put down; no big deal! You can avoid having to sign personally on a loan. If you follow our proven system, we can make it easy!" No, just no... Let me break down some of these lies for you.

<u>Non-Recourse Myth</u>

For a lender to get comfortable doing a non-recourse deal, they have to be reasonably certain the property can stand alone. Hoping they will be made whole if there is ever a default. Most non-recourse lenders will require a larger down payment, will have escrow requirements for repair & Maintenance, taxes and various other items. There is usually an occupancy and average rental rate threshold that needs to be met, and there will be limitations on distributions to the owners and to ensure the asset is not being drained.

In my experience, most of the projects you are looking at (as an investor) cannot meet these requirements. Can they eventually? Sure, but they are few and far between and require work. Over the years, I have helped several clients acquire properties that they were then able to improve and refinance non-recourse later, but not right out of the gate.

No Money Down Myth

As a consultant, this one really irritates me. I turn away a lot of clients who are trying to do no money down deals. I find it hard to take them seriously because, in my eyes and those of most bankers, they have no skin in the game. Often, they have unrealistic expectations making it very difficult to work with them. Understand that as a general rule, lenders are NOT going to do 100% Finance.

I am sure I will get some comment from some guy telling me about a time that he got a deal like this done. I call bullshit on this because they are probably not telling the entire story. They are the exception and not the rule.

Other factors played into their deal that are not mentioned. If a lender did a 100% finance on a deal, there were a lot of other circumstances around it that allowed them to get there. Depending on the asset type, they might lend 70-80% of the project. So how do you come up with the other 20-30%? That is where all these gurus with their magic systems come in.

Here is the pitch that you may get from the slick professionals in this space. They tell you ways to gather a group of "Passive Investors" who will give you all this money to buy this property. It sounds great, and these types of syndications do exist, BUT (big but) they are usually specialists for larger deals. They are also usually being run by investors with a lot of previous experience in those specific deal types.

In most cases, the potential investors, and the lenders are more comfortable if you have some of your own skin in the game. Is it impossible to put together syndication on a smaller property? No, but I am saying that a lot of these guys are selling you a line of crap that, "It will be SO easy to do."

Do Not Use Your Personal Credit Myth

As I did research to write this book, I read several other authors and articles written by people in my industry. I was hoping to gain a better understanding of the material out there and what was needed. Honestly, that is what inspired the title- NO BULL$HIT BUSINESS FINANCE GUIDE.

Unfortunately, these experts will try and sell you the biggest myth. One gave an example that if you went and got a business credit card with "Radio Shack" (I kid you not), it would build some history with your business. Your D & B Credit Score would go through the roof! Once this happened, no lender would ever ask you to personally guarantee a business loan again. I nearly threw that book across the room when I read that lie.

Now you might be able to get a business credit card or something similar under the business name, but usually, those will still require a personal guarantee. If you are going to take on any sizable debt for your business to buy equipment, real estate, working capital, whatever, you are going to guarantee that debt period.

I know these jack asses have testimonials of people claiming they used their magic systems and were able to get somewhere with it. I am more than certain that those borrowers are not buying a $1 Million building for their small business with no personal guarantee and with no personal credit check. They may have a $5,000 limit at Lowe's for their small business, but that is about it.

Chapter 3

From Sales to Banking

"There is no human problem which could not be solved if people would simply do as I advise." Gore Vidal

Who the hell does this guy think he is?

E ven though I believe I should wear a shirt with the above Gore Vidal quote everywhere I go, I know my wife would roll her eyes and say, "Bless your heart," while she handed me my honey do list. Marriage is one thing, but business is quite another. I have been in business finance for over 20 years and picked up the ins and outs of what banks look for in deals.

Now here is the part of the book where most authors tell you how it was their lifelong dream to end up in their profession. How they knew deep inside that this is what they wanted to do. I am not going to bore you with that because that was not me. I did NOT go into the field because I knew I would be a great banker. I did not even know it was an option for someone like myself. In essence, the field chose me.

At the time, I was doing well-selling investments and insurance. I was a young self-assured twenty-something year old kid with a new bride and a baby boy. Yes, the same wife that hands me the honey do list to this day.

Even with a fresh face and hardly any life experience, I was able to convince people as to the importance of life insurance and how they should manage their money. I loved reading and learning all there was to know about my field when I was not in the office. But like most eager men, I wanted to see what else was out there. I just could not see myself doing insurance forever.

One Sunday morning, while thumbing through the newspaper, I saw that a major bank was looking to hire business professionals with investment licensing. I decided to take the chance and interview. The candidates in the waiting room definitely looked the part of bankers. Some were older, clearly with more experience, while the others gave me glances of "this kid is in the wrong place."

When I spoke of my frustrations of not being taken seriously because of my age, my wife would always say, "You look young, but you talk like an old guy who knows his shit. Don't worry, honey. Your face will catch up someday". These days I wish my face had not caught up. I am now officially an old guy with wrinkles who knows his shit. It has gotten me where I am, so I cannot complain.

In the interview, I carried myself with self-assurance since I knew I had nothing to lose. Besides, I still had a good job in insurance waiting on me if these guys said "next." What I lacked was experience in banking specifically. I wondered how far back that would set me compared to the other candidates in the waiting room. It came as a surprise to me that my background in accounting, my licensing, and Business to Business sales (before insurance) actually made me stand out.

After a good while talking with the interviewer, the old guy sat back in his chair, stretched his arms behind his head, and nodded as he looked over at me. "You know what," he said as he leaned in, meeting me eye to eye. "It's crystal clear to me that you can sell. It doesn't seem to scare you in the slightest. You understand accounting, and you already have your investment licenses. That's pretty impressive. Now the banking part? You just leave that up to me. Son, I can teach you that part. It's easier to teach Banking to someone who can already sell..." Those words changed the entire course of my career.

It was the shift that made me a banker and propelled me to work with small to mid-sized companies. Helping business grow became a challenge that I was proud to do. I spent those years working my way up in the banking world. I was always eager to learn more on my own than what was expected. I wanted to get as much knowledge as I could to help my clients with their businesses.

After a few years' experience with that mega bank, I went across the street (literally) to another huge bank where I worked with relationship sizes up to $5 million. Because of the knowledge I was acquiring in the field; I was later asked to help launch a franchise lending division. I was learning and working in different areas of lending. That alone was exhilarating to me- I know it is weird.

Unfortunately, one of the challenges of working for a mega bank was the bureaucracy and tight credit box. I wanted more options for my clients, so I moved to more regional type banks (10 to 20 Billion in assets), where I spent most of my banking career. From there, I held several roles where I continued lending money to businesses from a few hundred thousand to $30-$40 Million and everything in between.

The more complicated the deal, the more I discovered that there were ways to structure it. I could finally sell The End Result. The selling of money never stopped, and I was glad to be that voice for my clients.

The career continued strong as I managed teams of lenders, approved credits, and was a voting member of loan committee at multiple banks. I received various awards and was even recognized as an SBA Financial Services Champion for the State of Oklahoma.

This is probably the point that you are thinking, "Why the hell should we care about all of this crap. What's in it for me?" Do I tell you this because I like talking about myself? You bet your ass, but I also tell you this so that you can be confident I know what I am talking about. I now have the honor of consulting businesses and finding them money every day. Only now I call the shots.

I will compare my background with any expert out there marketing books and programs for businesses in the space I focus on. I like knowing that people are succeeding in their businesses. The purpose of this book is to take you inside the mind of the banker and use what you can to make your loans and business work.

Chapter 4

The 5 C's of Credit Overview

"If you have a defined target you will have a better chance of hitting it," Bill King

As simple as this sounds, banks consider the elements of the 5 C's of credit when evaluating all financing requests. They are the basic building blocks to deals and clients. Each bank has their own variation of how they measure each area and what their requirements are, but it is consistent that each of the elements are considered. Here is a quick overview of the 5 C's to better understand what they look for. The following chapters will break down each C in further detail.

CHARACTER

Your banker is interested in how you have handled situations in the past. It shows the credit history of the business and ownership. I recommend you pull your own credit report before applying for a business loan. There are plenty of free resources out there that can provide you this information.

Be ready to explain any negative items on your report and provide supporting documentation if there is something you are disputing. I cannot stress how important it is to meet the obstacles head on and explain what happened. When they know the issues, they can better understand how to work around them instead of waiting for it to become a hurdle later.

In addition to your credit report, some lenders may even check the background of the ownerships of the business. They may even investigate any legal issues that might have occurred. There are several other items that banks will consider in evaluating character, but the bottom line is they are trying to get a sense of who you are. They are wanting to see if you a person with integrity that will live up to your obligations, especially when faced with adversity.

CAPACITY

Despite what you might have seen on TV or read in the newspaper, banks just want to get paid back. It is as simple as that. Capacity to pay is a measurement of your businesses ability to repay the debt based on historical financial information. In most cases, three complete tax years are evaluated and YTD (Year-To-Date) Financial Statements for the current year. In my experience, lack of documentable capacity to repay the debt is one of the most common reasons a small business loan is turned down.

Each lender has their own way of calculating Cash Available for Debt Service, but generally, they are taking whatever the net income/net loss of the business is and adjusting for non-cash items to come to this number. Some lenders use a simple EBITDA Calculation, and others will have more complex variations working through all the schedules of the tax returns, but the goal is the same.

They are trying to figure out if you can repay this loan based on what you have made in prior years, and each bank requires a cushion over this number. This is called the Debt Service Coverage Ratio, and as a rule, it will need to be greater than 1.25 Times your required annual payments. Again, there will be some variation by bank and industry, but this is just a guideline.

COLLATERAL

Okay, so the bank sees you have good Character, now they move on to another "C." They will look closely to prove you can repay your debt in the Capacity section, but what if you do not? This happens more than you think and is where Collateral comes in. It is then taken as a secondary source of repayment in the event the primary source does not come through.

Some of the things they look for are common types of collateral like commercial buildings, equipment Accounts Receivable, in general, all business assets filing, etc. Again, banks want to lend money, and they want to make sure they will be paid back.

From my personal experience, having managed lending teams and taking back collateral for loans that have not been paid is not something we enjoy doing. We will try to figure out other options before it must come to this. It is a pain in the ass but sometimes necessary. Usually, the type of collateral pledged will affect how long the loan can be amortized. Real Estate generally has the longest amortization, followed by Equipment, then Accounts Receivable, Inventory, and so on.

CAPITAL

While Capacity is generally a measurement of your businesses Income Statement, Capital is a measurement of the Balance Sheet of the Business and the Personal Financial Statements of the ownership/guarantors. A bank will take into consideration how much cash liquidity you have as well as your total assets and liabilities. A strong balance sheet and Personal Financial Statement can help a bank gain confidence that you will be more likely to handle the challenges if something goes wrong.

When you consider various times in history that sectors of the economy were hit, the businesses that were forced to file bankruptcy were the ones that took on too much debt during good times. They also had insufficient cash reserves to ride out the bad times. Although this is a generalization, the point is that a potential lender is going to take this into consideration in their decision for the loan.

CONDITIONS

This is probably the most misunderstood and frustrating "C" of business lending. Included in conditions are the overall economy, the local economy where your business/project is located, conditions in your given industry, and even the conditions of the specific bank you are working with.

For example, remember a few years ago when it was very difficult for businesses in the Oil and Gas industry to obtain financing? That was an example of a condition affecting financing. Many banks raised the standards of the scores required in each of the other "C's" because of the industry concern. Sometimes these inevitable turns happen.

Another example of a condition would be if a bank had a high concentration of credit or deals in an existing industry. A personal one that hit my own portfolio at a time were challenges obtaining Hotel financing even with experience and a strong flag. I wanted so much to help, but my hands were tied. No matter how strong the proposal was, the bank refused.

The reasons were that my bank had taken on many of these projects (hotels in my case) and did not have room to take on anymore. It is different for each bank, and sometimes the clients coming to us have no idea that this is going on behind the scenes.

Each lender evaluates these areas a little differently, but all areas are considered in most business loan requests. If your business is fortunate to check all the boxes perfectly, you will likely be extended credit on favorable terms.

In the upcoming chapter, I will try to guide you on what happens when you do not check all the boxes perfectly. Do not lose hope if you did not fit the C's perfectly. It happens to many borrowers. The good news is there are ways to work around it.

Chapter 5

The First C Is Character

"Our Character is what we do when we think no one is looking." H
Jackson Brown,Jr.

Dan Dan the Lyin' Man

I recently had a situation with a client that I thought had great character. My first impression was that of a hardworking, honest guy. My Spidey senses started to tingle with small things, like not being where he said he wanted to meet, missed calls followed by a long story, etc., but I took it as busy moment days.

The truth was, I liked him. I had gone to bat for this guy with lender after lender trying to find the right fit. After working together for almost a year (delays because of COVID), we were finally able to get his financing lined up. As we were going through the closing checklist, we discover he had several outstanding tax liens that he never told me about. Simply omitted them from our discussions.

Frustrated, I asked him point-blank, "Dan, you have to be honest with me. No more bullshitting. Are all of these taxes paid now? Do you just need to make sure the liens are cleared up?"

"Yes, Bill, I swear to you they are. I am in the clear," he said with certainty in his voice.

"Okay," I responded. "Because if there are issues, we have to hit them head on, so we know what we are working with."

He kept reassuring me that they were all paid. My gut felt off. Since we had been working together so long, I still went to bat for him with the lender and assure them that we would get it all taken care of. I become part of a team with my clients and work incredibly hard for them. I mean when I say- "I will fight for you and your deals."

Well, after more digging (damn the Spidey gut), I found out that some things remained unpaid. I was livid that this guy lied to my face. Those instances not only change how I perceive my clients but could also strain the relationship I have with my lenders. I work hard on building trust with them as well and want to only send them worthwhile people.

After that, I could not see Dan the same way. In my mind, I questioned every word that came out of his mouth. My belief in the kind of man he was no longer mattered. I did not see him as someone worth putting myself on the line for.

Now I understand that many of my clients have financial challenges and are not all Dans, but all I ask is they be honest with me. We can work around the challenges, but I must know what they are. I am here to present their case in the best way possible to potential financing sources.

Luckily, my lenders and I have mutual respect and trust after many years of working together. I was embarrassed, but the relationships with the lenders in Dan's case was not strained. The relationship with Dan? Well to that I say, "Good luck, and down the road, you go."

The No Bull$hit approach to Character

The first "C" is character. This is a common saying amongst credit executives in banking when discussing The 5 C's of Credit. After so many years, I see that phrase a little differently. It comes down to the gut-honest question of "Am I dealing with someone that is going to live up to their obligations? Or is this person simply feeding my ego by telling me what he thinks I want to hear?" This does not only apply to borrowers. I find myself gauging the character of ALL people I first meet. I deal with so many individuals and have discovered that not all are worth my time when I am working with them.

Whether it is a lender, a referral partner or a client, I have learned to rely on my gut. My wife refers to it as my Spidey Senses since she says my gut is full of chips and soda. She has a way of keeping me in check. Sometimes though (but not often), I am too wrong. Oh, how I despise being wrong.

Finding that someone was not truthful makes me more of a hard ass, but I still want to help people. If you have lied to me, I feel you have stolen time I could have devoted to helping someone else; it changes my perception. Nothing ruins the way I see a man more than that.

The lender needs to know if you are a stand-up person that will live up to your obligations. Now in this section, I get A LOT of people that have stories as to why their credit sucks. Everyday reasons like how their ex-wife screwed them out of their money, break the bank medical bills, a lawsuit, pretty much everything. But I get it; shit happens. We all have trials and tribulations every day that set us back. To understand your character, the lender wants to understand how you handled these past setbacks. Before I get ahead of myself, yes, they will look at your personal and Business credit management and ensure you do not have any legal issues.

There are even a variety of unwritten questions like: How does your personal credit look? If your score is low, why is it low? Have you filed for bankruptcy? If so, what is the story? How have you handled your obligations since then? Do you have back taxes? Are you in the middle of any type of litigation? The questions go on and on.

Do not let those uncertainties stop you. There may be ways to work around them but be upfront. Remember, the lender is simply trying to figure out if you have the character to pay them back. The main conclusion they are trying to come to is, "Can I trust this person?" If they feel they can, they will work to help you.

Chapter 6

Capacity/Cashflow

"We at Chrysler borrow money the old-fashioned way. We pay it back." -Lee Iacocca

Dude, I'll pay you Back.

As a teenager, I hung out with some questionable guys. They were the kind of people I prayed my own kids would never know. But most importantly, I hoped they would never come asking how their old responsible dad would ever choose as friends like that. Well, years later, I left my bad teen vibes behind and was a completely different person.

The day came when one of my hoodlum friends showed up one day at my doorstep. I was recently married, finishing up college, and was beat from working full time. We sat back drinking a few beers talking about the good old days of getting into trouble when he asked to borrow a couple of bucks. "Thanks man," he said. "I promise I'll pay ya back next week."

I did not think much of it. Sure enough, the following week, he showed up cash in hand, ready to pay up. I knew he was into some sneaky business that I wanted no part of. I was not sure how to say goodbye to my longtime friend.

A few days later, he came back again, the same deal of borrowing $50 or $60 bucks. Now at this point, my wife and I were saving all we could. Being newlyweds, we did not have much but made it work.

One night my friend came with the sob story asking to borrow $300. This was a lot of money for us that took a lot of time to save. We were in desperate need of a new washer, amongst other things.

My wife was not pleased, but I was confident my friend would pay it back.

The week came, and nothing. Two weeks turned to a month and then another. I knew that money was gone forever. I confessed my concerns to my wife.

"I'm so sorry, baby. It looks like the washer will have to wait. I just wish I had never lent him that cash," I said sadly, thinking of that money we had worked so hard to save.

She simply smiled as she took my hand, saying, "If it only cost us $300 to get rid of that no good sketchy guy and keep that fool from coming into my home, then it was worth it. There was something about him I just didn't trust."

He never came around again and even pretended not to see me when I would pass him in the street. For some odd reason, it suited me just fine. I realized that just like Bankers, I viewed Capacity for repayment and Character as one and the same.

Let Us Break it Down

The thing Bankers/lenders want is pretty simple. They want to know with a high degree of confidence that you are going to pay them back. Some of the things they look for are the following: In most loans, they will look overall at your last three years of business, personal tax returns, your most recent year-end financial statement, and how you are doing year-to-date.

Now, if this is a startup business or you do not have full three-year tax returns, there might be other financing alternatives (we will get into later), but it will be tougher. If you are buying some type of commercial investment real estate property or buying an existing business, they will ask for this information from the seller. Do not be surprised if the numbers provided are not that great.

In my opinion, the Capacity for Repayment is the hardest C to overcome and probably the most frustrating for borrowers. The challenge is that there is a battle between two major objectives of the business owner. I would argue that most business owners are interested in paying as little taxes as they legally have to.

There is a multibillion-dollar industry of Tax Accountants out there whose sole purpose is to make sure their clients pay as little taxes as possible. Am I saying that anybody is doing anything illegal, no of course not. So, if you are a CPA do not get your feelings hurt and assume that I am accusing you all of doing anything wrong; I am not.

Here are the reality bankers deal with. If your clients' tax returns show that they are losing money every year, that is a problem for most conventional banks and many private lenders. It makes their job tougher. How a lender calculates cash available for debt service comes into play. This will depend on the type of deal they are doing. A conventional bank will look at your most recent three years of Tax Returns to calculate your cash available for debt service. (Capacity)

Banks also ask themselves, "Was your business profitable for at least two of the last three years? What are the trends in sales and net profit, and how does EBITDA look? How much do you as the owner pay yourself, and what are your personal obligations?"

I know there are other so-called "Experts" out there that claim you do not have to guarantee these things personally, and if you are a "Corporation," you are shielded from liability, etc. I am here to tell you that is usually BS.

Typically, any person that owns more than 20% of a privately held company is going to be asked to guarantee the debt and provide personal financial information. Are there some sources that will not require this? Yes, BUT The financing is typically more expensive and more restrictive. Right now, I am talking about a conventional bank.

Different Business models and how Capacity effects them

Operating Business with a history

As I mentioned in the first chapter, the primary audience I am focused on are small to mid-sized businesses that have been around for at least a few years. That would be a particular category of borrowers. The lender is going to ask for your last three years business and personal tax returns and the current year interim Financial statements (Income Statement and Balance Sheet).

Every bank has slightly different variations of how they calculate cash flow, but one of the most common methods is looking at historical EBITDA (Earnings Before Interest, **Taxes, Depreciation and Amortization**). EBITDA margins help provide investors a snapshot of operational efficiency.

They will take the bottom line net income and add back Interest, Taxes, Depreciation and Amortization. This will give you what I call CAFDS (Cash Available for Debt Service). Then they look at all of your existing business debt plus the new loan you are requesting and calculate the annual payments for all of your loans known as CRFDS (Cash Required for Debt Service).

To get to a Debt Service Coverage Ratio, they divide the two, both CAFDS/CRFDS for each TAX YEAR being reviewed. In most cases, if this number is greater than 1.25, you will be in good shape for the calculation. If you are between 1 and 1.25 you and the lender may have something to work with. If you are below 1 to 1 it does not look as great.

The financials are telling the lender that you cannot afford to make the loan payments. It is at this point where most clients will disclose to me that they are making a lot more money than they show on their tax returns. Some even explain that they have been improving year to year and how NEXT YEAR will be greater. It does not bother me; remember, I want you to tell me about all the ins and outs. I know how it works, but it makes it more challenging.

Example

Here is what I have seen: There is a very common way that business tax returns and financial statements come in as they reach my desk. All three years of tax returns show a net loss or very small profit. Sometimes the EBITDA is reasonable other times not. For some reason, though, the YTD "company prepared" Financial Statements show a HUGE Increase in Profits compared to every tax year that we are looking at.

The borrower then asks, "Why can't we use my current year's numbers?" After I die a little inside, I answer calmly, "Because every small business owner we talk to shows a great profit with their internally prepared financials that seem to magically disappear when we get to the tax returns..." Okay, maybe I was never that subtle.

Remember, what you are, in essence doing is applying for the cheapest money available out there with a traditional bank. They are highly regulated and responsible for protecting the deposits of their customers while maintaining a strong rating with the FDIC (or other regulating bodies).

There is a lot they must think about. Could you imagine if they had loan files and were basing their decisions for the clients in quick-books financials? If that loan ever went bad, I guarantee you that bank would be in trouble.

The assumption that lenders must make, whether we agree or not, is that whatever you reported to the IRS is accurate (Stop laughing, I am serious). Am I saying that your loan is guaranteed to be turned down if you cannot demonstrate history? No, of course not. But we need to understand and recognize that to them; this appears as a weakness.

As I mentioned before, one of my pet peeves is when clients are not completely honest with me. In return, I promise to be honest with them, even when it is ugly.

As a lender or consultant, we need to measure your business in each of the 5 C's of credit and figure out where we are before we can decide how to proceed. If your financials show you cannot pay the debt, then that is what it will say if there is a story behind it, great. We can talk through that but let us not bullshit each other. We need to meet the problems head on, and the first step is sizing up how it looks on the surface.

Operating Business - Proforma Financials

Some people may ask: Do banks ever provide financing to operating businesses based on the cash flow of what the business will produce in the future, as opposed to what they have done in the past? Simply put-Yes. We might be able to find a lender who will look at projected revenue, BUT THE STORY HAS TO MAKE SENSE.

This is one area that I get really pissed off at with other people in my business. They try and sell the "easy button" to clients by saying "yes" without knowing the story or if the deal makes sense. If you are an existing business with weak historical cash flow, it will be harder to get conventional financing, period. We may be able to use an SBA Guaranteed program (which I will explain in detail in future chapters). Being able to get approval without a guarantee will involve other mitigating factors, but these areas need to be addressed.

Income Producing Real Estate with Historical Financials

The main focus of this section is investment CRE with deal sizes under $5 Million. Because these deals are usually made up of a small number of investors, typically require personal guarantees, and (unless) the property is very strong by itself, they require different attention.

Keep in mind another Bullshit calling moment- When you are buying investment properties for a hard to believe the price, there is usually always an undisclosed reason. I cannot tell you how many times I have heard, "Well, I know the rental income of this property is low historically, but the 'Market' rents are double, triple, what they are bringing in..." Yes, that is great, but as lenders, we still have to consider what the property has actually produced.

One of the good things about commercial real estate is that market rents based on a 3rd party appraisal are given a lot more consideration. If it is in fact, true that historical numbers are low compared to the market, we need to understand why.

The Truth calling moment here is- Most borrowers are seen as being unrealistic. You may be thinking, "I cannot believe he wrote that. How could you say that? Before you put the damn book down, here is the truth. People bring bullshit to lenders all the time.

Lenders are used to having every investor come and tell them that their deal is the best thing EVER. A few over inflated stories have unfortunately ruined it for everyone, making us as lenders leery of the content we are told.

If you can embrace this fact, then you can figure out what they truly want to know. Lenders are going to be skeptical of why you think you can magically make twice as much on this property than the previous owner. If you are completing renovations or have a new approach to marketing, etc., you need to explain the details and HOW you plan to make it better.

A borrower needs to show a property based on the projected revenue with supporting information on what will be done differently. Typically, the Historicals tend to look awful, so you as the borrower need to bridge the gap for us by explaining why. If the rental income is $10,000 per month and you are now going to increase it to $20,000, help us understand why it is doable.

Ground Up Construction - Income Producing

Income producing ground up construction is one of the few areas that dependence on projected revenue is generally acceptable. Keeping in mind that you are in line with market rents verified by a 3rd party appraiser. What I have typically seen on these types of deals is that borrowers under-estimate vacancy factors, management fees, maintenance fees, and how long it will take to get to full occupancy.

Chapter 7

Capital

"The amount of money that a person has in his bank account is not determined by his starting capital but by his knowledge about money and his ability to manage it properly." -- Sunday Adelaja

My first lesson on Capital and People

I will never forget my first slap in the face moment when I used to work for a CPA doing small business reorganizations. This was way back before I ever got into banking and in my early college years working as a junior accountant.

My mentor and I had had a client in the mattress business, and his books were a mess. We spent months in the pits trying to fix and hammer out our clients' finances. After many late nights, we were finally able to renegotiate deals with the IRS, the bank and his vendors to free up working capital. We figured out how to save his business.

Talking with the bank on past dues, vendors with the materials for the product while going back and forth nonstop with the IRS beefed up my negotiating skills. Life was preparing me for a career I could not have imagined at the time. Our long hours and months are finally seeing the light to help our client's business. I felt proud, but it was short lived.

This ungrateful client showed his appreciation with the biggest slap in the face to us both. Instead of taking that money (even part of it) and using it for his business, he instead chose to buy a more expensive house, a new luxury car, and other big toys.

Seeing the disappointment in my mentors CPA's face changed how I perceived that particular business owner. We were back to square one and expected by the boss man to keep fighting and finding him more capital. He did not even consider the work we had put in.

I discovered then that some people care more about the lifestyle and the perception of wealth. They make it a priority that the world "SEE" them as successful more than what is really happening in their business. They are lying to themselves, and sooner or later, it will come back to bite them in the ass.

Capital and Assets

It may come as a shock, but lenders look at BOTH your business and personal Assets (and liabilities). If you are reading this book, you are likely a privately held business owner, CRE investor or someone aspiring to be either of those. With that said, the Capital category is where a lender looks at your business balance sheet and your own personal financial statement.

While they seem like two different entities, in the mind of a banker, they are related when it comes to lending money. It helps give them a better understanding of you as a borrower. Think of capital as a combined balance sheet. You must consider the following questions as what a banker is looking for. Here is a quick rundown.

* How much in tangible assets do you have in comparison to liabilities?
* Are you already overextending personally?
* Do you have a lot of personal expensive toys?
* Do you have other business assets that can be looked at for additional income or collateral if something happens?
* How do your business assets compare to your business liabilities now and after the loan is approved (Assuming it is)?
* How highly leveraged are you personally?

Let me use the example that often happens in my line of work: An executive gets downsized. If they have been making $100-

$200,000 per year as a salaried employee for a big company and then go out on their own, understand that the bank will assume they will retain this same lifestyle. If their mortgage, car payments, credit card balances, etc. all are a drain- this must be taken into consideration.

That is one of the reasons most banks require personal guarantees on privately held companies. Banks know that most people will take care of themselves before taking care of the business. As bankers, we have seen it over and over, and it is always difficult to explain this to clients.

Chapter 8

Collateral

"Any other Collateral besides your heart of Gold and Million-dollar smile?" Randy Glasbergen

In this section, we ask the question: What are you pledging to the lender to secure the loan if you cannot make the payments? Here is the No Bull$hit truth. Despite what you see on the news, read in the newspapers, or see on social media, lenders ARE NOT excited about throwing grandma out of her house or throwing you out of your business. We can all visualize the picture of the fat cartoon banker lighting a cigar with a dollar bill as he watches orphans and grandmas freezing in the street.

I have yet to personally meet someone in my industry that gets pleasure from this act. Unfortunately, I have had to take back a business (building, equipment, etc,) as a Loan Manager. Even though I am considered a hard ass in my field, there was nothing I hated more. People are losing their dream, and the bank having to take it back, no thanks. That is not part of banking anyone is proud of, no matter how we may be perceived in stories and movies.

There is a saying in banking, "No one can sell anything for LESS than a banker." You may need to read that quote twice to fully grasp its meaning. How does that apply to those in my field? Well, as a business owner, if you could not sell the asset and we must take it back, it is usually sold for pennies on the dollar.

Some consider the buyers that purchase these types of assets from banks as bottom feeders. No offense, bottom feeders, I have been one myself for my real estate business, and it has served me well. All we are doing is trying to get the most for our money, and if that means being called a bottom feeder, I have no objection. We have tough skin and know when to buy.

These folks know that if the bank has taken it back, they want to get it off their books as soon as possible. The bank has already written down a portion of their losses and continues to write down their losses every month. Having the non-money-making asset on their book is not something they want.

Now that I am done with my outburst on the nasty side of taking back a business, you can see why collateral is important. The lender needs to clearly understand what assets are being pledged as collateral for the loan request. The type of collateral being offered has a great impact on the amortization of the loan. **Amortization** simply means: How long you have to pay the loan back.

If commercial real estate is your primary collateral type, generally, the amortization can be 15-25 years. Yes, sometimes it can go as long as 30 years, but that is generally limited to Multi-Family or a collection of One to Four Unit Residential rentals.

If the primary collateral is Equipment, the amortization is typically three to seven years. On the other hand, if the primary collateral is Accounts Receivable, Inventory, Good Will, etc., the amortization will be shorter than that.

In some cases, you might even have a revolving line of credit with interest-only payments and an annual renewal. If they were to term that out, generally the maximum term will be three years. So, different collateral varieties call for different Amortization schedules.

Varying types of collateral also allow for different Advance rates (Loan To Value). An advance rate lets you know how much a lender will give you on the collateral type. For example, in Owner Occupied Real Estate, you might have an advance rate of 80-85%.

Investment Real Estate is made by 60-75% depending on the type of real estate and if it is a special use property. I will explain later in the book the different types of CRE and what a Special Use property is for those in that space.

On Equipment deals, though, depending on the structure, you can find sources that will do 100% financing. I have a whole chapter on Equipment Leasing/Financing that gets into this detail. If you are working on a traditional bank loan secured by Equipment, though expect to put 20% of your own money down.

Inventory typically will have an advance rate of 50% on finished goods and will exclude WIP. Sometimes Raw Material can be used as collateral. While most C & I Lenders will give you 75-80% on Eligible Accounts Receivable.

On certain types of lines of credit, you will be restricted by what is called a borrowing base report. I have an example of this in the appendix for your review if you have never used one. The line is usually secured by Inventory and Accounts Receivable. Most commonly, your advance rate will be 50% of Finished Goods Inventory; if Raw Material is a commodity type item, you might get 50% on that, and WIP will be excluded. For the Accounts Receivable advance rate, you will typically receive 75-80% of "Eligible receivables."

Some of you may lose your mind here where I explain what eligible AR truly is. If you have any one client that makes up more than 20% of the total AR balance, a portion of that account will be excluded. (Typically, the amount in excess of 20%).

If you have any AR that is over 60 days past due, they will be excluded. Lastly, if you have an account that has a large percentage over 60 days pasts due, this account can be considered "tainted," and any balances due from this client could be excluded. Remember, I am talking about a competitively priced revolving line of credit here. If you need more money than this, there are other options, but they are expensive.

Chapter 9

Conditions

"I am interested, but it all depends on the terms and conditions."

-Grant Dalton

Sometimes things occur that you have no control over. They are a constantly changing element. This applies to not only the economy as a whole but the economy in your local area. These pesky things known as Conditions are not always under our power yet affect the world around your business.

Stupid Covid lockdowns are a great example, but there are other less obvious ones as well. There are cases where the client has great credit and nice historical cash flow. They are strong and might even have a solid balance sheet and money to put down on their purchase.

The business checks all the boxes, and BOOM! They still get turned down. But why? This does not make any logical sense. In many cases, this can be attributed to the fifth C- Conditions. Many different factors outside of your control impacts this.

For example, one might be in the Oil and Gas business, Hotel Operator, or even a Restaurant. The only downfall- They are in a business that is not desirable to the lender/bank they are talking to. Sometimes, it is as straightforward as that. I have seen dozens of examples of industries that some lenders shy away from while others need more concentration in those fields.

Oftentimes certain industries are known to have a higher default rate and while others may show some type of declining trend that makes the bank leery. Unfortunately, that is what happens in a lot of banks, but most will not admit it.

If you are in the construction business and you are doing progress billing, keep in mind that these lines will be harder to get. Ask yourself these questions: Is your industry a high-risk industry for this particular bank's credit box? Think back on the credit box discussion from the first section. Is the overall economy weak? How you tell your business story matters here.

As of the writing of this book, we are in the middle of the COVID crisis that has caused many banks to tighten up their credit policies. The pandemic will also be taken into consideration as part of the approval. This is one of the reasons that I went into this line of work. I know it is hard. I want to help borrowers find sources of financing if they are having trouble with their local bank or they simply would like representation in making sure they are getting the best deal in the process.

Another bias and Condition I would never have considered is the "Never again" guy. I observed different forms of these occurrences in my career. As a seasoned member on the loan committee, and had a bad experience in his field 20 years ago. He internally vowed to never do one of those types of deals again. So anytime an opportunity was placed before him in committee, he shot it down. No matter how clean the deal was, he could not wrap his mind around it because of the bad experience. Not everyone is this way, but it does happen.

In addition to industry concerns, there could be uncertainty in the market you are trying to do business in. Is it fair? Of course not, but that is why making sure banks know the entirety of your story is important. It could very well be the balance that tips the loan in your favor.

Chapter 10

Cashflow Cycle and Working Capital Financing

"Money is a guarantee that we may have what we want in the future. Though we need nothing at the moment, it ensures the possibility of satisfying a necessary desire when it arises. -Aristotle Wrap

Your Business Will Always Need Money

I love running my own business and calling the shots. I told my wife the other day, "I'm lucky I don't have to worry about getting fired, but my new boss is an asshole."To my surprise, she agreed and said, "It's true. Plus, he's always coming on to me." Yes, she was talking about me.

As an entrepreneur, I know a part of me has become unemployable. I had a hard time listening to people that wanted to control my way of running things. The constant reminders of "who is in charge" began to wear on me.

The difference now is that even though I listen to what my clients and lending sources have to say, it is because we are working on a unified goal. We chose to work together. That is the opposite than working for someone who felt a need to call the shots to simply to put me in my place.

If we business owners want to keep these roles, we need capital to do it. It is as crucial as choosing the right partners. I am hoping this next section serves as a wake-up call and guide on what to expect.

And now for a shocking sentence that needs to be read twice-
One of the top reasons businesses fail is they grow too fast and can not keep up with their cash flow cycle.
For the purposes of this chapter, Net Profit- DOES NOT Matter. Paper profit does not equal cash in the bank, particularly if your clients are large companies or, even worse- the government.

Top line sales are great and profitable accounts are awesome, but you have to respect your cash flow cycle. For my fellow finance geeks reading this, do not kick me out of the club because I will be providing a simplistic outline of a cash flow cycle. This is intended for the guys that do not wear pocket protectors like me.

Here is a manufacturing example to provide an illustration.

1. **You have to buy raw material**- Depending on the relationships with your vendors, you will have to pay cash or have accounts payable for this.

2. **Work In Process**- You will have expenses in labor, material, utilities, etc., in converting your raw material into finished goods.

3. **Finished Goods**- They are complete and ready to sell but sitting in your warehouse.

4. **YOU MAKE A SALE**- Your company finally got the big kahuna account that you had been trying to get for months. This is a new relationship, and the sales guy promised flexibility in repayment terms to get in the door. He gives you some BS that it was "really competitive" and "The other guy" was cheaper. Luckily, you were able to win it based on terms. Unbeknown to most people, this happens every day. In reality, we do not even know if the other guy exists. Remember, purchasing people are taught to squeeze salespeople for the best price and terms they can get.

5. **Product ships and waiting on payment**- You now ship the product and are supposed to receive payment in the next 60 days. I will add in a few scenarios and upsets that may come into play during this time: The customer claims they did not receive all the items. In some cases, claiming that a few of the

items were damaged, and they decide to hold up paying the complete invoice because of it.

The accounts payable department only processes payments on the first and the 15th, and your payment was not technically due until the 2nd or 3rd of the month, so it will not go out until the next batch on the 15th. Betty the AP clerk, is out on vacation for a week, and no one can get that payment processed until she gets back. There are a lot of reasons your payment can get delayed. These mishaps do happen in our imperfect business world.

6. **You receive payment!** Realistically you will receive full payment by 75-90 days out if it is a bigger company in this scenario. Before you lose your mind and tell me that you have the best collection process and all your payments are complete in less than 30 days, consider yourself lucky. Many businesses do not have that luxury.

This example shows what I have seen time and time again. Hundreds of business financials in this scenario are more common than most people know. If you are the exception (I truly hope you are), your cycle will be somewhat shorter.

Quick Sample Calculation

Here are examples of specific calculations based on your financials. To calculate cash flow cycle days: Let us say (for this example) it is 60 days. After taking into consideration that some of the vendors are giving terms on your orders. Your business has $1 Million in sales per year with a COGS of 60% that is $600,000 annual or roughly $50,000 per month. The fixed cost shortfall in your cash flow cycle is about $100,000 in this example. The question is: How do we bridge that gap?

In a perfect world, you have a great relationship with your community bank, big bank, whatever, and you have already been in business for a few years. They will collect the financing package from you and run through their approval process using the 5 C's of credit. Here is how they will typically be analyzed in something like this.

You Reach the Next Step

So, either the lender approves you, turns you down, or asks for more information. More times than not, you get back a huge list of questions. In most cases, your deal is probably already dead, but surprisingly enough, your loan officer may not know it yet.

Sometimes it is just inexperience, or they string you along with hopes that it will go through. So, the question becomes: What do you do for working capital if a regular bank line is unavailable? Luckily, there are more options out there than most businesses are even aware of. I specialize in this area and have provided my services to clients for years now as we navigate the right fit.

1. SBA Guaranteed line of credit

SBA Express is commonly used for lines of credit. Keep in mind that not all banks offer this, so I may have to take you somewhere else to get it set up. Think of this type of SBA loan as an insurance policy for the bank. You are still receiving the funding from whatever lender you are working with or another source I can take you to. Fortunately, the SBA is going to guarantee it after we jump through all of the hoops. Do not let the name "Express" fool you. The process is a little faster than other SBA loans, but come on, we are dealing with the federal government here. These guys can screw up a two-car funeral procession.

Do not misunderstand; I love the SBA. They help provide access to businesses that would otherwise be turned away or must pay a lot more for financing. But the process can be a big pain in the ass. Working in this area, I will not sugarcoat it. I have done hundreds of SBA loans over the years, managed an SBA team, and was even recognized by the SBA as a financial services champion. So yes, I know my way around this beast.

If you are needing to navigate this process, it is a good idea to get professional help or at least make sure you are working with a bank that knows what they are doing. Not all banks have someone on staff that specializes in this, so be careful.

2.Other Options

If you decide not to go the SBA route because you do not have the time to wait, are uncomfortable with SBA, or simply do not qualify, then know there are still other options. Assuming you have good accounts receivable from businesses, there is an option called an ABL facility. This stands for Asset Based Lending Line of credit. It looks like a regular line of credit but with a few distinct differences. ABL facilities are available through both bank and non-bank sources and are typically much more restrictive than a regular line of credit.

When you look through the 5 C's of credit, a lender in this category will accept weaknesses in industry, credit, capital, and maybe even cash flow, as long as there is a good story. Remember, they are focused more on the quality of your clients and your company's ability to perform the services/provide the products.

They are typically more expensive than a bank line and usually have a lockbox or total control account requirement. This means they will have some control over your bank accounts. I know you do not like giving control to anyone, but keep in mind it may be a small price to pay since you are the one that needs to borrow the money. Sometimes the give and take need to be there.

3. Factoring Facility

The factoring industry has gotten a bad rep over the years, but I really appreciate the segment of the market they fill. Like any industry, there are some bad seeds, but on balance, these guys provide a needed service to help small businesses expand. I recognize and value what they do for companies so much that I became a member of the International Factoring Association.

I researched and worked with several reputable companies in this space to help my clients. All parties have been pleased, and I expect more businesses to lean in this direction for help. But as I said, be cautious- There are some bad players on the field.

Within the factoring world, there are certain lenders that favor particular industries and types of clients. For example, if you are in the construction business, you will have a hard time finding a source. Luckily, I do know a few.

Another one that is hard to find is in the Medical Factoring space. If your clients are smaller businesses, there might be challenges to finding a good source, but not impossible. The easiest types of borrowers to take to factoring companies are businesses that sell to strong, established companies.

In essence, what a factoring company is doing is buying the receivable from you. They pay an advance rate upfront and charge a discount fee. Then the remaining balance will be paid to you when the receivable is collected. The good thing is there are a wide range of pricing models to explore.

There are several ABL and factoring lenders out there that only work through third party consultants like me. A normal business owner would never even know about most of these. A lot of what I do when I take care of a client is try and find two or three sources that I think would like their deal. Then, I negotiate the best terms that I can.

I had a client in the manufacturing space that we set up a $3 Million factoring facility for. We were able to replace another factoring service that I felt was overcharging them. The annual savings to this client was over $200,000.

Not only are they are getting a hell of a deal, but they now have a better partnership with the new company. My consulting fee was well earned in setting up that relationship and saving them thousands upon thousands.

4. Inventory Financing

There are not a lot of sources that are non-bank lenders and will lend on inventory, but there are a few. It can be very expensive and typically will be partnered with a factoring line. I have some sources that do this, but they are pretty particular on the quality of the inventory that will be pledged and a lot harder to get.

5. Purchase Order Financing

I get asked for this financing a lot. Unfortunately, if you are a service business, using this kind of financing will be virtually impossible. It is also hard in the construction business or has any type of milestone or progress billing. Manufacturers, distributors are providing some type of tangible product based on a solid contract; we may be able to find financing in this area.

There are some services that offer this in addition to factoring and standalone PO Financing companies that will then partner with the factoring company. If you are interested in this, let me know, and I will see if I can help you since it is a hard road to navigate.

6. Merchant Cash Advance

Even though I hate these types of deals, I feel I should make you aware of their existence. This would NEVER be my first choice, so caution if you decide to go this route. These guys may be able to help if your business does not have business accounts receivable, you cannot get bank financing, and you need working capital. They are typically looking at your bank statements for the last few months and estimating the available financing based on that.

One of the things to be careful of with this type of financing is that they generally do not say they charge "interest." They instead claim to charge a fee for short term financing. They usually have short maturities of 30-90 days, and their "Fee" can be 1-3% per month.

If you have a short term need that WILL NOT BE RECURRING, these guys can be a great resource. Where you get killed is that once you dig into the hole, you cannot get back out. The trap is set and nearly impossible to overcome. I have talked to countless clients that fall into this trap and remain stuck. I feel for them, but there is not much I can do to help at that point.

Let us say you are a restaurant, hotel, retail store, etc. (Warning- these are all favorite targets for these guys). You borrow $100,000 for 30 days, and it costs you $2,000. You find that does not feel too bad. Then when the loan comes up for renewal, you are short on cash again. Your MCA person tells you, "Hey, no problem, just pay us another fee, and we will extend it for another 30-60 days." It is not always what it seems.

They often require access to your bank account, so their payments come out no matter what. They get paid first, making it is very hard to pay your other bills. Here is an example and some quick math.

You are in the restaurant business (I feel for you guys because it is always hard to finance restaurants and even tougher now with COVID). Your net profit is probably 5-10% if you manage your labor and food costs well. If your cost of capital jumps to 24% annually and your profit margin was 10% before taking on this additional expense, what is your profit now? Yes, you are now losing roughly 14% and digging yourself into a hole.

It has to continue, and you are out of luck. Am I saying there is No place for MCA lenders? No, BUT you must know what you are getting into. Do not let them Bull$hit you into thinking it is easy and cheap because it is not.

7. Unsecured Alternate Financing Sources

If you do a google search of small business financing, you will find plenty of brokers out there promising unsecured loans for up to $250,000 bad credit, no credit, we don't care, blah blah blah. I never bother to deal with these guys at all. Since I provide consulting in addition to loan brokering, I am called on constantly by other brokers peddling this crap, and I just shoot them all down. My old guy experience has been if something sounds too good to be true, it probably is.

I am a firm believer in the basics of the 5 C's of credit and the fact that anybody who is lending money is expecting to get paid back. If someone promises great rates with no collateral for a business with a weak cash flow history and a borrower with bad credit- I just cannot buy it.

I have yet to see a client obtain any meaningful financing through these types of sources. They usually end up being some type of MCA structure, as referenced above, or it is turned down. If you can find something in this area, more power to you.

The Guide has Spoken

I am certain there are other creative financing sources out there. One of the things that I do when I am consulting a client is looking at their financial statements and figure out what we have to work with. Maybe they have equity in equipment, a building or something else that we can leverage up. I am able to look into what they may not see.

The most important thing I hope you take away from this chapter is that even if you get turned down by your specific bank, there are other sources out there. Remember that every bank and/or credit union has their own credit policy.

Although they all consider the 5 C's, they underwrite a little differently. Never forget that using an SBA guarantee helps widen the net for many of these lenders of what they would consider. Beyond that, I have non-bank sources that can get more creative until your business is strong enough to qualify for more conventional type financing.

My hope is to help you assess where you are now, find you the best terms available (given your situation), and then bridge towards better financing options down the road. You can do this. Your business is worth it.

Chapter 11

Equipment Finance

"The top experts in the world are ardent students. The day you stop learning you're definitely not an expert." Brendon Burchard

"**H**oney do you want all the little letters after your name on these newsletter mailouts?" yelled the wife as she helped with some clerical work from her office. If anyone can set me back to a humble state, it is her. I swear she does it on purpose.

As mentioned in my Bio, I am a Certified Lease Finance Professional **CLFP** (the little letters the wife mentioned). What that designation means is that I have several years' experience in the equipment financing space and have taken a battery of tests certifying my knowledge in that field. Not many Brokers or even lenders have that designation, but if I wanted to do the best job for my clients, I better know what I am talking about. So those damn letters are a big deal.

When I started these important facts to her, she smiled and simply stated, "So, YES it is. Thank you, husband," and continued typing. She definitely does it on purpose.

As with any professional designation, we have ongoing Continuing Education requirements. Do I tell you this because Bill likes to say how great he is? Again, yes. I want you to be comfortable that I have a good handle on what I bring to the table.

There are many misconceptions regarding equipment financing vs. equipment leasing, so I am going to try my best to dispel some of the myths as I walk you through this. Equipment is a broader term to include furniture fixtures and equipment. Most businesses require some type of equipment to operate and provide services.

I have financed everything from phone systems for clients, office furniture, manufacturing equipment, medical equipment, even construction equipment. The list goes on and on, but lately, the most unique for me was helping three business partners buy a plane. Now that was a fun deal.

It is unfortunate that the equipment finance industry is misunderstood by businesses and even by many banks. Here are some of the basic structures of obtaining an Equipment Loan to help in your industry.

1. Regular Bank Financing

From a pure interest rate perspective, this will be the lowest cost but will usually require a larger down payment. For round numbers, let us say you are buying $100,000 piece of equipment. Assuming you check all the credit boxes for your bank, they will ask you for 20-25% down (depending on the age and type of equipment), and the typical amortization will be 36-60 Months. They might go longer in some cases if the equipment is new and has a longer useful life.

I am talking standard bank policy here, not the other "Let me talk with my manager" scenarios. I can already hear some of you moaning. "But Bill, I heard about my cousin Joe who got his bank to finance 100%..." Yes, that does happen, but it is generally an exception and not a rule in bank policy. Cousin Joe had other things in his finances or portfolio that made him look desirable to that bank. I am sorry to break it to you, but not everyone can be Cousin Joe.

2. Equipment Finance Companies (Both Bank owned and Non-BankOwned)

There is a difference between a regular bank loan and financing through their Equipment Financing/Leasing Departments. The first and most important thing in my mind is that providing 100% financing on the equipment (plus another 10% for soft costs in some cases) is NOT a Policy Exception.

This is important because for a regular bank to give you over 80% financing, there must be additional strength in your deal that allows them to do this. With an equipment finance company, it is strictly part of the standard underwriting.

Bank Owned Equipment Finance Companies have tighter credit requirements and focus more on what we call A-B paper. Your non-bank equipment financing sources are all over the map, which can be a good thing. You can find sources willing to do deals from A-D and startups in some cases.

The biggest difference is the cost of funds. I will save you some time and say this: If you are expecting very low rates and expect to have no money down, that is going to be a hard combination. You might try a bank's equipment finance division and see how that goes.

One of the interesting things in Equipment Finance is that they usually will not quote you a "rate." What they will do is give you a Payment Amount and Term. Here is a basic outline for you below the three basic types of financing structures in the Equipment Financing world.

For my fellow CLFP's and Equipment lenders that might be reading this, please cut me some slack if my details are not exact. I am providing some broad-brush explanations for our users and trying not to put them to sleep.

A. Leases

Oh No, not the world Lease! Slow down there are relax. Lease is not a bad word. Remember as a business owner; you need to be more interested in preserving cash for operations and getting to use the equipment right now. It may go by several other names, but an operating lease can accomplish both of those objectives.

Let us use this $100,000 Piece of equipment as an example. Under an operating lease, there will be a residual value at the end of the term that is like a balloon on a loan payment. Usually, they will calculate the "Fair Market Value" at the end of the term, but for this example, we will just say it is 20%. It is the minimum value for it to technically count as a true lease. So, you would be financing the

$80,000 balance over, let us say 60 months, and then have the residual value of $20,000.

You could either trade the equipment in at that time, pay it off, or see if the Equipment leasing company would amortize the remaining balance over another 12-24 months. This is pretty common.

In this scenario, you get the lowest monthly payments and use of the equipment for 60 months while you decide if you want to keep it. You then have the option to buy it at the end of the period. You will not technically own the equipment during the lease period, but who cares. The fact that you are getting to use it matters more. The lease payments should be tax-deductible. For clarity, you can confirm with your own CPA regarding the tax treatment for your specific business.

B. Capital Lease $1 Buyout

It may come as a surprise but, in Capital Lease Structure, you are committed to the full balance of the lease is spread over the term. If we were using the same $100,000, 60 Month example, the payments will be calculated based on the $100,000 amount with a $1 Buy out at the end.

In this scenario, you would still not own the equipment until the end, but the assumption upfront is that you intend to buy it. Tax treatment on a Capital Lease is usually similar to an amortizing loan. The payments will be higher than a comparable operating lease, but you do not have to worry about a residual amount due at the end of the period.

C. An Equipment Finance Agreement

Not all Equipment Leasing Companies offer this, but an EFA is pretty much a 100% Loan to purchase equipment. This structure is best for a client that feels a need to have the pride of ownership from day one but still wants to put as little money down as possible.

Some may be thinking, "Bill why would I want to do this when I could just get a bank loan the same way?" As I had mentioned earlier, an EFA is available through both bank and non-bank lenders. Providing 100% financing is not a policy exception in this case AND they can get comfortable with weaker credits than a bank will. If you want to have the pride of ownership and your bank will do 100% finance, I say take it.

*Disclaimer: Any general information here regarding taxation is for discussion purposes only. We do not pretend to be CPA's and recommend you talk with your own accountant about the tax ramifications of any of these options. We are happy to be a part of that discussion if you choose to hire us as your consultants.

When looking at Equipment Finance from an underwriting perspective, Equipment Finance companies pay attention to the quality of the equipment to be pledged as collateral, and the equipment needs to be essential to the operations of the business. There are some exceptions to this, but that is a general rule.

Although they consider all of the 5 C's of credit, it is my opinion that underwriting in this area focuses more on the collateral than the other C's. If you have strong collateral and have weaknesses in other areas, you might still be able to put a deal together. Note that in this space, you have specializations by industry and equipment type. Many lenders/leasing companies will say that they are "generalists," but most have types of equipment and industries they prefer over the other.

Challenges

One of the challenges I have seen with borrowers who have never dealt with equipment finance before is the hang up on the Effective Interest Rate. For example, a $100,000 Capital lease for a strong borrower might have payments of $2,055.60 with no money down required or maybe one payment upfront. That payment would equate to an interest rate of roughly 8%. Bank pricing for this same deal, assuming you could get the bank to do 100%, might be 5%, and the payment would be around $1,915.27.

If you leased this same equipment using an Operating lease at the cost of 10%, the payments would be about $1,891 with a $20,000 residual. That breaks down to a difference of a little over $100 per month. In the scheme of things, it is not very much.

Disclaimer: *Source of these examples are T- Value calculations under the three different scenarios. These are for illustration purposes only.

Advantages

Another great advantage of Equipment Finance companies versus conventional banks is Turnaround Time. That means the money in your pocket sooner. Assuming you have your ducks in a row, they can get a smaller deal funded in a couple of days and larger deals in a few weeks.

For many clients, the quicker process is worth paying a little higher rate. Every equipment deal is different, and every business situation is unique. It is a good idea to work with a professional when you are considering buying equipment.

I tried my best not to go into too much of what my wife calls "The Banker Talk" in this chapter, but sometimes it is necessary. She cleaned up as much as she could (being co-author), but sometimes the numbers must speak.

My hope is to give you a better understanding of the examples listed. It is not going to be an easy process which is why there are people like myself to navigate you through the complexities. Those little letters at the end of my name sure have taught me a lot.

Chapter 12

Commercial Real Estate Overview

"Let us never negotiate out of fear. But let us never fear to negotiate." John F Kennedy

I can represent myself. Um, let us reconsider that.

Here is a dirty little secret about MOST real estate deals. The commission of 5-6% is going to be paid in full whether you bring in a realtor to help you or not. If you are considering leasing or buying, I highly recommend you find a good commercial real estate professional since there are a lot of moving parts. I work with several throughout the country and would be happy to recommend a few if needed.

I had a deal recently where my client was buying a car wash. Unfortunately, by the time it got to me, the borrower was already in contract and did not hire a Commercial Realtor to assist him. There were several things I noticed in the contract that a good commercial realtor could have negotiated for my borrower. He honestly did not know better and did not realize he was getting stepped on.

The selling agent was a real piece of work, and I saw it right away. This SOB agent was making a full 6% on the deal and, in my opinion, did a very poor job of representing his seller. I had enough and found myself stepping in on my buyers' behalf.

I reminded this agent that the challenges of this deal were property specific and that my client was rock solid. After throwing out legitimate facts on the deal, I also, in a kind tone, reminded him that I knew plenty of commercial real estate companies with properties similar to this one that would love my client as a buyer.

Yes, my asshole mode kicked in. But as most people know, I hate when I see people being taken advantage of. He backed off.

How do you pick a good commercial Realtor?

As you know from reading other parts of this book, I respect people who take extra steps to obtain designations and training in their professions. One of the designations in the CRE space is a CCIM (Certified Commercial Investment Member). To qualify for this designation, you must take several courses, demonstrate a certain level of experience and pass a battery of tests. For more information on the details, you are welcome to go to CCIM.com. https://www.ccim.com/about-ccim/what-is-a-ccim/

One of my friends, Angela Harwell CCIM here in the Dallas area, is an advocate for buyers and commercial tenants and gave me great insight into this chapter. Let me tell you; this woman is incredibly knowledgeable. I work with Angela's team and several other experienced commercial Realtors here in DFW and nationwide because they have what I am looking for.

What I require is simple- good character and responsiveness in taking care of clients the way I do. Whether you select a CCIM or not, I encourage you to seek out an experienced COMMERCIAL real estate Professional- Not a residential Realtor that "Can do" commercial.

Do not get me wrong, Residential real estate people are awesome at what they do, but a VERY small percentage understand what goes into a commercial deal. Even in the commercial field, you would probably be better served to select one that has experience with the specific asset type you are looking at purchasing/leasing.

I am not saying that I have any problem with the Selling Agents, BUT their job is to represent the seller of the property, not the buyer. I know there are situations where they act as an "intermediary." They then represent both sides but, in my opinion, it is very hard to do. Get your own tough dog in the fight, and it will be a lot easier in the long run.

To Buy or to Lease? That is the Question.

There are a lot of different opinions on whether you buy or lease your location. I am including a link to a great article below from the CCIM website that provides some additional insight into it.

https://www.ccim.com/cire-magazine/articles/lease-versus-own- decision/?gmSsoPc=1

I include the link because this is a situation that constitutes great debate in my field. The direction you choose to go depends greatly on your financial situation, your liquidity, and how confident you are in the location. Then ask yourself if the plans are to keep your business long term. Either way, there is usually a financing need.

Different Types of Real Estate Deals and General Financing Info

The major difference in underwriting capacity for repayment between Owner Occupied and Investment CRE is the source of income to the property. Generally, an Owner-Occupied deal will be more focused on the success of the business even if you hold the real estate in a separate entity and lease it to yourself. With Non-Owner Occupied CRE, the primary source of income/debt repayment is from rental income of the property. Whether it is owner occupied or not, the type of property being purchased can also influence the way the deal is structured and if it is approved.

General Guidelines for Different Property Types.

Raw Land –

If you are buying raw land and do not plan to develop and build on it immediately, most lending sources will require more money down and will usually have a shorter amortization. When the economy is down, this area of financing seems to tighten up a great deal. The biggest challenge I see with investors looking into buying land is the expectation of a lower down payment. It is not uncommon to have lenders require 35-50% down on raw land deals where there is not an immediate development/construction plan.

Development Financing –

In the business, we call this "Horizontal" work. The finished product will be either residential or commercial lots that can be sold to builders, or the investor can build on them. Generally, less money down is required than raw land by itself, and you are going to be limited to the lesser of your cost or appraised value. Lenders become more comfortable if you have more experience and have had previous developments.

Construction Financing –

I am including both residential and commercial here, BUT I am not talking about you building your own house to live in. For residential, I am referring to building houses to sell or lease. This type of financing is generally easier to find than land and development. It is still more limited than financing for existing completed buildings. Again, you will be limited to the lesser of cost or appraised value.

1-4 Family Rentals –

There are several lenders that like these types of deals, but their pricing and terms tend to be all over the map. Fair Warning- please do not call me with the 100% No Money Down Financing BS.That to me, is a pipe dream. I know there are a lot of people selling potential investors on this BS every day; rest assured, we see through it.

If you are serious about investing in this type of real estate, or any for that matter, expect to have some of your own money in the deal. Financing is typically limited to the lesser of your total cost or As Repaired Value (ARV).

I run into borrowers every day that say, "Well, I am buying this property for $100,000, but it's really worth $200,000. All it needs is $10,000 of work." No, please stop. If it was really worth $200,000 THAT is what you would be paying. There are a few lenders that will not restrict you to the lesser of cost or ARV, but they will typically be very expensive while the LTV is lower.

Multi-Family –

Similar to 1-4 Family, there are plenty of lenders that like the multi-family space. Whenever the complex is five or more units, the underwriting shifts to Multi-Family and becomes a commercial deal.

One of the biggest challenges I have seen over the years is a residential investor that is used to terms in the 1-4 family world is now trying to do their first Multi Family deal expecting the same.

I have been known to turn a potential client away. I simply do not have the time or patience to argue with them about how much "They think" they know regarding how the process will work and the terms they expect. I always leave the door open when they to go out on their own, get kicked around a little bit, and come back after a reality check. That stays in the past, and we simply move forward.

Within the commercial world, multi-family is the most similar to residential. There are cases where one can get amortizations up to 30 years, depending on the property age and condition. The down payment and variable rates most seen in multi-family deals are usually the biggest shocks for investors transitioning over.

In most cases, you will be expected to put 20-25% down on a project, and your typical fixed rate period will be three to five years (if it is Buy and Hold Financing). If you must do a "Value Add," there is usually a bridge loan needed while you get the property repaired and stabilized. Then a couple of years later, we can take it out with more competitive long-term financing.

"True Commercial" Properties that are not Special Use

What I mean by True Commercial are properties occupied by businesses- not residential. I have seen three major categories in this group that would not be considered special use. They are office, retail, and industrial. As of the writing of this book, Office and Retail sadly are taking a big hit with COVID while the industrial sector has taken off.

Office –

Just like it sounds, it is primarily office space. Most of these spaces may have a warehousing component and a reception area, but most of the square footage is dedicated to offices. Lenders will generally allow for a lower down payment if it is owner occupied VS investor real estate.

Retail –

Depending on the nature of the retail business, this property type can shift into special use. For simplicity sake, let us look at this as a regular strip center. Moving one tenant out and another in will not require major renovations-as opposed to a bookstore becoming a restaurant.

Industrial –

There are several types of businesses that fall under the industrial umbrella. One of the largest growth areas over the last few years has been E-Commerce. I mean, think of how many things you have bought on Amazon or at another online source over the last few weeks.

Generally, Industrial spaces will have a larger square footage dedicated to warehousing and/or manufacturing & production. They tend to have higher ceilings and are not intended for walk in customer traffic. In some of these spaces, there may be a small office area or retail storefront, but most of the space is dedicated to industrial use.

Special Use Properties (in General)-

When you are dealing with a property type that has a limited selling area like a Hotel, Mini Storage, Car Wash, Restaurant, Gas Station, it would be considered special use. They would be very expensive for a buyer to convert it to something else. Remember that from a lender's perspective, the whole point of having collateral is to provide a secondary source of repayment if you fail to perform. The lender must consider what the marketability of the property will be if they were forced to take it back.

Your potential buyers will be operators in those specific industries. These buyers know that if the bank owns it, there was a problem. Based on these factors, most lenders will require a larger down payment from the borrower on special use properties to make up for this additional risk.

That is one of the reasons that SBA guaranteed loans are very popular with special use properties. You might even get away with a lower down payment (assuming you check most of the other boxes in the 5 C's) using an SBA loan.

Pros and Cons of Lease Spaced from a Financing Perspective

Typically, the landlord will give you some build out allowance to help you modify the space to your needs. You will need to pay for the remaining leasehold improvements yourself either with cash or a loan. Being you do not have any ownership rights to the property, the business loan is unsecured for all intents and purposes.

When a client is moving into a new space, they are either launching or growing their business. I will cover launching a new business in more detail in another section, but you will likely need an SBA guarantee for that.

If you are expanding your business, you might be able to qualify conventionally but may be able to receive more favorable terms with an SBA guaranteed program. SBA loans are used in one of two ways. They either help you get approved for a loan when you otherwise would have been turned down, or it can help you receive more favorable terms than what I bank would normally offer.

In this example, let us say you had a $500,000 Loan request for new equipment, build-out, permanent working capital, etc. If you have a strong business, you might be able to obtain a conventional bank loan. The bank would likely want to see that you have put in 20% or more into the project, and the amortization would be three to five years, depending on the exact collateral. Those type of payments can be a real strain on cash flow.

If you use an SBA 7A loan for the same structure, a lender may allow up to a 10-year amortization and possibly as little as 10% down on the project. This can preserve some of your capital up fronts and lower your payments.

Chapter 13

Purchasing Owner Occupied VS. Investment CRE

"The problem with Real estate is that it's local. You have to understand the local market." Robert T. Kiyosaki

I thought all real estate was the same.

Owner Occupied Commercial Real Estate is probably one of the most desirable types of loans for most banks. The exact definition of "owner occupied" varies some, particularly if you are using an SBA loan. As a rule, if you occupy 51% or more of the property, it is considered owner occupied by banking standards. If you have an established business and have been leasing space for a few years, considering a real estate investment may be a good idea.

Over the years, I have had many borrowers referred to me that had already been turned down by a bank (or two) and were coming up on the end of their contract period. After reviewing the financial statements, I could tell within ten minutes if they had tried to buy more than they could afford. Other times they needed more time to find the right financing.

Remember that lenders look at the Capacity for repayment when clients come to them. Traditional banks look closely at those deals keeping in mind Historical Tax Returns. There are ways to use projected income, but that takes a little work and probably the use of an SBA or USDA program (depending on the location).

I always recommend that a business owner have his financial statements evaluated by a professional before taking up a lot of Commercial Real Estate professional's time. It is important to have a handle on what you can really afford and what type of loan structure you can qualify for before shopping around town for the right project.

One of the things most people run into when buying commercial real estate is whether the property is considered Special Use or General Use. Why would that be important information to know? If you are purchasing an Office/Warehouse, light industrial or retail space, these properties usually qualify as General Use and would not be very difficult to modify the space for another user.

The same would apply if you were a landscaping company in a light industrial space and you moved out. It would not be too hard to get that same building ready for a trucking company to use. Special Use is a little different.

With a Special Use property, it would require renovations to be used for anything other than its current use. Some might require major renovations and used differently if it was converted from hotel to restaurant (for example).

Other examples of Special Use properties are Hotels/Motels, Restaurants, Car Washes, Mini Storage Facilities, and Auto repair shops. As you could see, if the lender had to take a hotel back, they will likely only be able to sell it easier to someone else in the hotel business. The market of potential buyers is limited.

Special Use properties will require larger down payments and probably have a shorter amortization if you are working with traditional banks. We can use SBA/USDA programs if the property type qualifies.

Conventional Loan on Owner Occupied properties are usually 80% Loan-To-Cost, so you would have to put 20% down. If the property is Special Use, a conventional lender would limit you to 70-75% Loan-To- Cost, so you would have to put 25-30% Down. Amortization on the property will be 15-25 Years, depending on the age of the property, if it is special use, and if the bank has an appetite for that asset type.

If the deal qualified for an SBA program and you decided to go that route, you can get away with as little as 10% Down. Keep in mind that the lender may require more depending on the situation.

Whether you go SBA 7A or SBA 504, your amortization can go as long as 25 years, regardless of property type.

This is a prime example of a situation where the borrower may qualify without an SBA guarantee but request terms that a bank would not be able to accommodate without a guarantee lower down payment and/or longer amortization for example.

My Recommendation:

Many of my clients have had success owning the Real Estate in a separate entity from their operating company. This allows them to keep the asset as a separate income-producing entity. Down the road, if they decide to sell the business, they can continue to own the real estate and lease it to the new owners. If you choose to go this route, you need to speak with your tax adviser with regard to structuring it this way. Fortunately, I have seen several like this over the years.

Income Producing Real Estate with Historical Financials

The main focus of this section is investment CRE with deal sizes under $10-20 Million. Because these deals are usually made up of a small number of investors, typically require personal guarantees, and (unless) the property is very strong by itself, they require different attention.

Another Bullshit calling moment- When buying investment properties for a hard to believe the price, there is usually always an undisclosed reason. I cannot tell you how many times I have heard, "Well, I know the rental income of this property is low historically, but the 'Market' rents are double, triple, what they are bringing in..." That is great, but as lenders, we still must consider what the property has actually produced.

One of the good things about commercial real estate is that market rents based on a third-party appraisal are given a lot more consideration. If it is in fact, true that historical numbers are low compared to the market, we need to understand why. If you are planning on renovations, different marketing, on site management

VS absentee owner, etc., you need to explain the details and how you differ. Remember, lenders cannot help but feel skeptical until they are comfortable with the deal and know you will be managing the property better.

One more aspect that drives me nuts is when a borrower shows a property based on projected revenue with nothing to back it. I then ask for historical, and more often than not- they look like crap. You, as the borrower presenting your case, need to bridge the gap for us. If the historical rental income is $10,000 per month and you are going to increase it to $20,000, you must walk us through it. Make us understand why the projections will be believable.

Ground Up Construction - Income Producing

Income producing ground up construction is one of the few areas that dependence on projected revenue is generally acceptable- As long as you are in line with market rent verified by a third-party appraiser. What I typically see on these types of deals is that borrowers under-estimate vacancy factors, management fees, maintenance fees, and how long it will take to get to full occupancy.

Chapter 14

Non-Franchise Start up

"Don't sit down and wait for the opportunities to come. Get up and make them." Madam C.J. Walker.

I want to start my own business, but now what?

A startup and non-franchise business is one of the hardest types of financing. I promised you No Bull$hit, so that is how I am going to start this chapter. I speak with people all the time who tell me they have wanted to start their own business for years. I have heard stories of how frustrated they are with their jobs and how much they want to be their own boss.

Sometimes I will ask, "How much money have you saved towards starting this new business?" Usually, I am met with the same answer. They will tell me they have not had a chance to save anything yet. They are valid reasons like, "You know with kids going to school, we just bought a new house. We are getting another car..."

We are hitting the basics for those wanting to start a business. Another question I generally ask is if they have decided what type of business they want to start? While some claim not to know, others have a definite answer. If they do know, I follow up with, "What training and research have you completed or started in preparation for going out on your own? Have you set up your entities? Have you started expanding your personal credit availability? Are your scores high to prepare for revolving credit to help with your personal needs while you get the business off the ground?

I may suggest they go to the SBDC or SCORE to start putting together a business plan and cash flow projections. I usually discover that certain people are not really serious about starting a business yet; they just like the idea of not having someone tell them what to do.

There is a Chinese saying, "Don't wait until you are thirsty to start digging a well." I view the idea of going out on your own the same way. It is much easier to qualify for financing while you have a stable source of income (through either yourself or your spouse) to get the business off the ground.

One of the most frustrating things for me as a broker is to work with Community Development lenders who are supposed to be here to help small businesses get going. Unfortunately, they can charge a higher rate on SBA loans than other lenders because they are a nonprofit. They market themselves as doing deals banks will not do. Sorry to say, most require startup businesses to cash flow and, in most cases, not from the business at all. That makes the situation harder, becoming a double edge sword. It becomes more challenging to keep the current job before starting.

I recommend getting the business going as much as you can, leading and setting the foundation. Treat it as a side hustle testing to see if you are even going to like it before jumping all in. Nothing is worse than starting on a path that you soon discover you do not even like.

Most sources I have spoken to have said the only way they can do a startup deal is if the borrower has outside income. This is EXCLUDING THE PROJECTIONS FROM THEIR NEW BUSINESS to service the debt and pay all their living expenses. These community advantage lenders, micro lending investment people, and whoever else can THEN charge more interest than a regular bank.

The Example

Here is an example of how that conversation might go with Joe and the Micro Lender:

"So let me get this straight; I have been a machine shop worker for ten years. I have gone out on my own and started my own machine shop, but you will not help in provide me financing because I quit my job to start this one? Is that right?" Asks a completely baffled Joe.

"Well, does your spouse have a job?" The micro-lender asks.

"No, not anymore. She left her job to work the business with me."

"And you no longer have your old job?"

"Right. Plus, I couldn't stay at my old job because I would be considered a competitor. It would be a conflict of interest if I worked both. We invested our last dollar into this. We just need a little help," Joe answered.

"Oh, well, I'm terribly sorry, sir. But we cannot do that loan. That's not how this works..."

As frustrating as these conversations go, the bright side is there are some lenders that can work with you even though they are hard to find. I know a few, and we do plenty of business to serve people like the ones mentioned above. If you have not started your business yet and still have a day job, here is what I would encourage you to do.

1. Create an Entity for Your Business

It does not cost a lot of money, and you can do most of these things yourself without an attorney. I set up our company several years before we really went into this business full time. You can do this by registering with the Secretary of State and then check with the County for an assumed name.

2. Research the Field You are Considering

The success rate for business owners who go into fields they already have experience in seems to be higher than going into a totally different industry. The exception to this rule might be using a franchise model because they can give you a framework of how to get started and proceed. If you are not going to go the franchise route, consider something related to what you know.

3. Work with your Local SCORE or SBDC Office

They will help you research the businesses you are considering and put together a basic business plan and cash flow projections. If you cannot make the time to put together a business plan, projections, research, then you are considered not truly serious about going out on your own. They are there to guide you. Running your own business is a grind, and the better you prepare, the better chance you will have of succeeding.

4. Start Putting Money Away and Expanding your Available Revolving Credit

One of the most irritating things for me to see is someone telling me they have been wanting to start a business for years but expect someone else to 100% finance it. If you have no skin in the game, no one is going to take you seriously. Banks, lending sources, and possibly other entrepreneurs will see it as simply a pipe dream. It is not going to be easy, but you must work for it.

5. Start Keeping Track of what you are Investing

If you are spending money on training, research, office equipment, etc. while you are getting ready to start-Keep these receipts. Depending on the financing structure, you may be able to count some of this as your contribution to the project.

I had a deal where a borrower came to me and said he needed $300,000 to open up his new business. I asked, "Okay, how much are you putting in?" He said, "I want a bank loan for the full amount." Before I told him "Hell No" and chased him out of my office, I decided to dig a little deeper (those Spidey senses again).

As it turned out, he had already done a lot of homework and had already invested a sizable amount in tools, equipment, training and research. He had spent about $100,000 in total.

I encouraged him to re-frame his request to something like this: "The total project is $400,000, and here is an itemized list of the $100,000 I have already invested. I am requesting $300,000 in additional funds to launch my venture..." Now that is a very different story. Do not misunderstand; it was still a tough deal to get approved, but it had a lot better chance under that structure.

6. Review your Current Household Expenditures

Figure out how much you really need to keep bringing in when you go out on your own. This is one of the most overlooked areas for a startup business. When I left banking, I was walking away from a six-figure income and knew I was not going to replace that overnight.

Fortunately, I am working in a field that I was already experienced in. We had planned for this move, but it was still a tough transition. I have spoken to many business owners who left executive roles to go into business for themselves and discovered that this was a huge challenge for them as well. So, save, budget, and prepare as much as you can.

7. If Possible get an SBA Loan

Before you are full-time out on your own try to see what you can get. This goes back to my rant above. There are financing sources out there that can do SBA loans with projected revenue- But to come out stronger, you will have a lot more options available if you have other sources of income. Having a buffer will be detrimental as you are working on getting paid from your business.

Chapter 15

Buying an existing Business

"It is hard to believe that a man is telling the truth when you know that you would lie if you were in his place." H.L Menken

The good, bad, and ugly of EBITDA

I may upset some of my Business broker/Intermediary friends in this section, but some things must be said. If they are anything like me, they have tough skin. They know as well as I that this is not an easy career. We know the difficulties that exist in this world and recognize that it is not for everyone.

There is a high likelihood that as a new business owner, you are going to need an SBA guaranteed loan. In most cases, there is almost never enough tangible collateral in relation to the sales price. The cash flow is seldom strong enough to cover payments on a short amortization. Now, for the No Bull$hit part.

When a client is buying a privately held non-franchise business, they are usually dealing with a situation where the owners want to retire. Perhaps something happened to one of the partners, and the other partner has decided it is time to move on. There are dozens of stories as to why businesses are up for sale. Sadly, the sales price is almost always inflated as it relates to the actual historical cash flow the business had produced over the last few years.

One of the challenging things about underwriting a business purchase is that half of the financing consideration comes from the seller and the other half is from the buyer. Here is what I mean. We are interested in your credit as a buyer, your character, your experience, your financial capabilities to make the down payment and sustain the business transition. We will also look at your personal balance sheet and the assets of any other businesses you might own. The other half of the information comes from the business being sold.

In order to make a strong assessment of what we have in front of us, we as lenders/consultants ask ourselves-

* *How has the business performed?
* *Are the trends improving or declining?
* *What are the tangible assets that are being included with the purchase?
* *Will the seller be available for transition?
* *Will the seller consider a carryback note behind the bank loan if there is a short fall?

EBITDA

An important term to get familiar with if you are looking at buying an existing business is "Adjusted EBITDA" or "Seller's Discretionary Earnings." In layman's terms - Earnings Before Interest, Taxes, Depreciation and Amortization with modifications the seller is asking to be added back.

To us as lenders, that could mean the historical financials are probably weak, showing a declining trend, net losses and the EBITDA right off the tax returns is probably not sufficient to cover the debt.

The "Adjusted EBITDA" takes into consideration all of the "Add Backs" of expenses that you as a buyer would not have to deal with. For example, Mr. Seller pays his deadbeat cousin $50,000 per year, but he does not really contribute much to the business. You can get rid of him, and boom, you have a $50,000 add back.

The seller might also say he pays a lot of personal expenses through the business. He pays his car, insurance, groceries, whatever, and that is another $50,000 add back. The seller's salary, well, he has paid himself $100,000 per year, and you (the buyer) only plan to pay yourself $50,000 even though you just left a job that pays a lot more than that.

As the new owner, the buyer is probably going to be very energetic. He will probably want to do a lot of things the previous owner did not, all with the hope of increasing sales dramatically. After all the adjustments, the company that has shown historical net losses of $100,000 suddenly is $250,000 to the positive.

I am being a little facetious with this example for the sake of making the point that, in general, sellers are going to claim the business is making more money than the financials show. They are going to demand a higher price than what the assets reflect. With all of that said, does it mean you should not buy the business? Not necessarily; I am just preparing you, the reader, that this is a common challenge on these types of deals.

Although I can and do finance these even with all of these challenges, as an individual, you would probably have a hard time getting the deal done on your own. Most buyers do not know all the elements that come into play. The things I look for in business purchases like these are a buyer that at least has 10% to put down and a seller that is willing to consider a carryback note for a portion of the deal if necessary. I also look for the buyer to have transferable experience from whatever they were doing before trying to buy this business.

Personally, if I sense that we have a seller (or the seller's broker) that is inflexible and not willing to come to a fair agreement, I will generally pass on the deal and let someone else take a swing at it. Sometimes people just will not budge. It is then that I must decide if they are worth my time.

Chapter 16

Business Buying Another Business

"The entrepreneur always searches for change, respond to it, and exploits it as an opportunity" Peter Drucker

M & A Transactions (Mergers and Acquisition)

I am often asked the question, "What is the difference between an M & A Deal and a regular business purchase?" The major distinction, in my opinion, is that you have an existing business buying another business.

Let me rant for just a moment. One of the biggest pet peeves I have in this space is: If you are creating a company to buy an existing business, BUT your existing business has no historical performance, you my friend, are a Start Up.

With that said, do not call and try to "interview" me like you are a hotshot. Coming at your possible lending sources as if they will need to fight or prove that they are worthy of working with you will get you nowhere. Come down from your high horse until you learn to ride.

I have encountered many people like his and see right through the bullshit. I have found that most of the time, they are Start Ups. It is always a welcome surprise when I meet one that is not, but those are few and far between.

They usually do not have a lot of money to put in, very little experience in the field, but still manage to have a big ego that is very hard to work with. As expected, I do not mind letting those go.

Okay, now back to M & A deals. These do not have to be entirely huge publicly traded companies we see in the media that gobble up little businesses. I realize there is a misconception about this and know this is not the way most of the companies operate.

In this example, let us say you are an established plumbing company with $10 Million in sales. You see an opportunity for growth. You might have a chance encounter to buy a smaller HVAC company that has roughly $3 Million in sales. Plus, their business complements yours, and it is seen as a good move by both parties.

The underwriting for the financing of this type of request will usually consider the historical financials of BOTH companies along with the projected revenue of the combined entities. I had a deal some time back where I was helping a manufacturing company buy a smaller business that they could then absorb into their operations. Due to the reduced overhead and several other synergies, the projected net profit was improved overall. It was a different way of doing it, but it worked for that scenario.

Chapter 17

Behind the Curtain of The Credit Process

"I feel like I'm putting together a jigsaw puzzle. I have all these pieces of history of his story. And I'm trying to assemble them into a complete package." Gayle Alvarez

What is included in a Complete Loan Package?

The number one question I get asked by borrowers and business partners is: Bill, what does a "complete loan package" include, and why are they asking for all this stuff? Let me give you an example of what the dialog is between the borrower and lender is when this question comes to play. Remember, the more you know, the better prepared you will be when your time comes to meet with them.

"Well Mr. Lender, I have been banking with XYZ Bank for ten years. I've been a good client but am now ready to take out a loan for my business," says Mr. Borrow.

"That's great to hear. We at XYZ Bank consider ourselves 'Relationship Bankers.' We like to serve our clients with the fastest and most efficient turnaround," replies Mr. Banks, sitting back in his chair as he scribbles something on a notepad.

"I'm so glad you said that. Now, how long does this process usually take? My business sure could use that money soon," Asks Mr. Borrower...

Now let us pause for a moment because we are about to get into the portion of the conversation that drives most borrowers and referral sources nuts. As a recovering banker, I have gone through this same discussion hundreds of times. The banker is about to say

SIX WORDS that you as a borrower do not fully hear or may not completely understand. Know it is not your fault!

We as bankers, have done a poor job of defining these six words. Quite honestly, we sometimes must change them in a case-by-case scenario. Sometimes our underwriters will even change them for us. Let us continue our conversation and hit on those six words...

"That is a great question Mr. Borrow. **Once we have a complete package**, we will finish the approval process in one to two weeks. We may be ready to close in 30-45 days depending on third-party reports, etc.," replies Mr.Banks with a reassuring smile.

Mr.Borrower walks out of that interaction thinking that all he needs to do is send Mr.Banks some basic information, and boom, his deal will be turned around in no time.

Bill's Bull$hit Alert

If this is a full doc deal of any size and they tell you it will be a few days, they are probably being overly optimistic and trying to get your deal off the street. Also known as trying to make sure you do not shop it to another bank, or worse- a guy likes me before they get a chance to look at it. I am here to tell you that over 75% of the time, things WILL NOT turn around as fast as you think they will. Here is why.

The mysterious six words that make the turnaround long are **"Once we have a complete Package."** The borrower will usually get a checklist from the banker of what they routinely need. These things will include the last few year's tax returns, a personal financial statement, and information on what you are planning to use the money for. They may require a more detailed list, but this is the gist of what you will be asked. There are typically four-five parties involved in the initial process, and chances are you will never meet the most important one. The people included are you, the banker you are dealing with, a market executive (on larger deals), the back-office underwriting department, and the final decision-makers (Credit Exec, loan committee, etc.). The underwriting and approval levels will vary depending on the size of your deal. If the deal is small and is scored, a lot of this would be automated.

I typically dealt with loans from a few hundred thousand to tens of millions. In this space, there will usually be a credit analyst/underwriter type that is working on the file. Believe it or not, the analysts/underwriters are my favorite people and the MOST IMPORTANT people in the credit process.

I mentioned my belief in this in the section "Inside the Mind of a Banker." Their job is to protect the bank from the sales guys up front like myself and the people I used to manage. Right or wrong, that is how many of them view their job. They are typically very analytical and believe in having complete and correct information before proceeding to the next step.

If you have ever studied DISC, Meyers Briggs, Enneagram or any other personality analysis systems, these guys are the Conscientious, analytical, methodical type but damn good at what they do. One of the downsides is that, unfortunately, they are generally stretched way too thin.

Banks expect so much from these folks. Depending on deal size, bank structure and various other factors, underwriters can each be handling deals from a few lenders up to ten at any given time. Every Lenders deal is a rush, and every one of those is supposedly the most important, needing to be handled right away. The kicker is, almost every loan package is considered incomplete by the underwriter's standards.

Chapter 18

Why Your Deal is Taking So Long

Hot potato is a very different game when the people playing are starving."Demitri Martin

The Damn Hot Potato

This is where the real breakdown happens in the commercial lending process in my opinion. Let us say your typical underwriter has ten deals assigned to him from the que. They will be all different in size, project types, collateral structures, and all coming from various officers.

They almost always have a backlog of five to ten projects AT LEAST. Their supervisors judge them on how complete their write ups are, how many deals they get through, and the quality of the work they are doing by screening out deals the lenders never should have sent up.

The easiest visual I can use to demonstrate this is imagining their loan files as Hot Potatoes. If you have ever played hot potato as a kid, the objective is to touch the potato for as little time as you must before passing it on to someone else. Using that analogy, what typically happens is your deal is waiting in line to EVEN be looked at by an analyst for several days. The initial review of the file is usually triggered when you call the loan officer to ask what is going on.

They call/email the analyst who cannot help but get irritated because they are working on two to three other "rush deals." They stop what they are doing and look at what the lender has sent to them on Your file/deal.

If they find anything missing that they thought the file should have or anything that looks out of place that triggers more questions or requests for additional information, guess what they do? They send the hot potato back to the lender.

It will usually be in the form of an email saying something like this: " Banker guy, I noticed your borrower has scheduled E income from other entities, and I don't see those in the packet. We will need the complete tax returns of everything feeding into the return to review the file." Or other things like- "The borrower only supplied two years of tax returns, and we need three, The borrower did not include their COMPLETE tax returns only the first few pages, The borrower didn't sign their PFS, and so on. These are all legitimate things that take the responsibility off of them and puts it back on the loan officer to track down what they are asking for.

So what happens now to the damn potato?

The loan officer is busy working on several other projects, managing his/her portfolio, taking care of renewals, technical exceptions, and so on. He receives the reply from the underwriter. He will either forward the email from the analyst directly to you, or he will cut and paste what the analyst said into a new email to you asking for the information.

This is where you, the borrower, now lose your mind. You may yell at the screen or say this to yourself, "I gave you all of this information two weeks ago! Do you mean to tell me that you are barely looking at it for the first time only to discover there is more information you need to even GET STARTED?"

Now take a deep breath. Hopefully, you have not thrown this book, your tablet or your phone across the room as I touched on a painful nerve. Any borrower that has gone through this can completely relate to what I just described. The answer to your question is yes, that is exactly what just happened.

I know I will have my loan officer friends saying that they are different, and their bank is much better and more efficient. That is great, but I am telling you from 20 years' experience, having worked in various banking environments as an executive and as an independent consultant, this happens every day. But the fact remains- What can we do about it?

The only thing that we can really control is understanding from the beginning of what the Credit Analyst/underwriter defines as a COMPLETE PACKAGE FOR THIS TYPE OF REQUEST, and I hope that this scenario will be avoided.

There will be some basic items that are required in most deals , and there will be other items that vary. I am providing a link below to a free checklist and explanation of items to help you provide the most complete and organized package possible.

Remember, we are directing these efforts to the most important person in this part of the credit process- the Credit Analyst. He/she is the one who will help move your deal across to the finish line.

Here is a link to some free resources we offer our clients, including a free checklist
https://www.NoBullShitBusinessFinanceGuide.com/No-BS-Free-Resources/

Chapter 19

Building a Complete Package Up Front

"It's not about how to get started; It's about how to get noticed."
Steve Case

H ere is what you need to get your deal noticed.

Deal Summary – Think of this as a cover paragraph or two explaining your project. When I am training groups on this subject in my workshops, I tell the audience to imagine you are sitting down with someone in a coffee shop, and they ask you to tell them about your project. *What are you requesting the loan for?* It sounds simple, but this will overcome writers block that stumps people as they prepare to write their summary. For example, let us say you are buying a commercial building for your growing business.

Your deal summary might be something like this: *XYZ Widget Company has been in business here in the DFW area for five years. We have been fortunate to grow steadily and have outgrown our current lease location. We have identified a building and are interested in for price of $2 Million. We expect to spend another $500,000 on renovations. Out of this $2.5 Million total, we are requesting financing of $2 Million and will contribute the remaining $500,000 to the project* (sources and Uses of Proceeds).

Side Note: You must understand that as Bankers, we have looked at so many deals, and we are mentally checking boxes and looking for red flags as we read through your deal. I feel more confident in a deal when the questions are clearly answered by a borrower or their consultant in this basic write up.

You can then mention what your company does in summary and how the new location will benefit your business. State the highlights of your financial trends and detail about the building itself.

WARNING – Do not go into too much detail. Talk about just a few things so not to lose the banker. I promise there will be a place for more detail later.

I usually write my deal summaries last. I will get into the details of all the elements in the body of the memo and then come back up and summarize it in a cover sheet. What I used to tell my lenders when I trained them on writing credit memos was to use the deal summary to highlight all the major items and direct your more analytical readers to where they can find more details.

Give them the facts.

If you have multiple businesses, keep in mind that we are focusing on the primary operating entity of the company that needs the loan. I will get into a section later where we provide additional information on other businesses that feed into your personal tax returns.

What is needed is three years of complete business tax returns. Although it sounds super simple, you would be surprised how hard it is sometimes for borrowers to provide what is needed. I am often told, "Other lenders say only need two years? Do I have to provide the whole returns? Can I just send the first few pages?" or a myriad of other questions.

This basic request is often non-negotiable and will set your loan back if we are not given what we need. Again, this book is focused on Privately held businesses that have been around for at least a few years, so three years of tax returns is not unheard of.

In 99% of the cases when you are applying for financing over $250,000 this information will be requested. The less complete the information is, the lower your chances are of getting approval and the higher your rates are going to be. Historical tax returns, for example, are used at conventional banks and for SBA loans to calculate your Capacity for repayment.

Do not forget about those 5 C's of Credit from the previous sections. Remember the lender examines those tax returns to look at your ability to repay. They evaluate your personal and historical tax returns to get an estimate of not only the profitability of your company but your personal income from the business and other sources. It describes the history of your business, and it is all about telling the complete story.

Most conventional banks refer to themselves as "Cashflow Lenders." What that means to a business borrower is that the primary source of repayment they are looking at when making a credit decision is that the business operations are supported by the owners personally. If your historical tax returns show a net loss (as many do) and your EBITDA is not sufficient to cover this loan. Any of the other existing obligations you have outstanding, will need to be tackled upfront.

Here is a link to some free resources we offer our clients including a Personal Financial Statement Form at
https://www.NoBullShitBusinessFinanceGuide.com/No-BS-Free-Resources/

Income Statement and Balance Sheet

You will also need the most recent year-end business financial statements. Most business owners I work with sometimes file extensions for their tax returns. I have even done it myself for my personal business. What that means in this case is that for the year, the most recent year-end tax returns have not been filed. So that will lead us to look at company prepared financials.

Let us say it is August 2020, and you are bringing me a loan request. The most recent tax return you will have filed is usually going to be 2018 because 2019 returns are on extension.

To analyze how the business is trending, the lender will look at your year-end and YTD (Year to Date) Financial statements, but this will not be the entirety of the basis of how they calculate your ability to repay.

A common story which I bet is familiar to most business owners reading this book is having year-end tax returns that all show net losses. Sometimes two out of three years have net losses. When the EBITDA is looked at, we notice some add backs for depreciation and interest. Unfortunately, even that number is small.

Let us say EBITDA is $100,000. The year-end financial statement for the current year shows a net profit of $400,000 when all prior years were negative. Typically, a lender will note this as a positive trend but will not use this as their basis for showing you have the demonstrated ability to pay this loan. That does not mean your deals dead in the water. You might need someone like myself to help you navigate the process. Again, year-end Business Financial Statements are needed to analyze how your business is trending. They help answer the questions like:

* Are your sales going up or down?
* Does your business have seasonality?
* Are your profits increasing or decreasing?

Together they tell the story of your business, but more importantly, how it is favoring.

The Credit analysis is trying to predict where the lender thinks the company is going based on where it has been. If there is any major jump or drop in a category, they automatically begin to ask and wonder why.

As I mentioned above, the mind of a commercial banker is series of mental boxes that need to be checked. If the information being reviewed creates more questions than answers, your request will likely have more challenges.

Chapter 20

Getting them to YES

"The ability to see the situations as the other side sees it, as difficult as it may be, is one of the most important skills a negotiator can posses." Roger Fisher

You are almost there.

There is a saying in sales, "A Confused Mind Always Says No." You have to understand that your credit file is, essence, a sales presentation. We want to get a yes from the people in the bank that approve writing big checks to business owners. The individual you are dealing with on the front line usually is a salesperson. I mean no offense because as most know, I admire that title. They might have some credit skills, but they are seldom the decision-makers. Luckily, they do influence the decision and are a great advocate through the process. But there is almost always somebody else that gets to say yes.

In most cases, there are several layers of people that have the "yes" power. As I mentioned earlier, the main person we are focusing on will be the credit analyst/underwriter. The goal is to help them check all the boxes in their heads to help get our loan approved.

We want the analyst to get comfortable enough to feel it is a good package. We need to think as they do, so ask yourself questions like: *If there was a big change year after year can I explain why? Why did Sales Jump 30%? Did our repair and maintenance expense double? Why did that happen, and most importantly, do we expect it to continue to be higher?*

I learned how to answer this by analyzing church and nonprofit loans. Nonprofits normally do not make any money, so how can they pay a loan back? Well, in general, what is done is we look at their sources of income and then at the expenses.

The way they look at expenses is different. They are separated into "Discretionary" and "Non-Discretionary" categories. For example, a church has rent to pay, utilities, salaries to core employees, etc. -I would consider these Non-Discretionary expenses- meaning they must pay for these whether the church is doing well or not.

Discretionary expenses are different. Think of nonprofit income like -Use it or lose it money. Being a nonprofit, they must use the money for something, and it has to be in line with the course of action for the organization. If the church has extra money, they might go on a mission trip somewhere, as an example. They might even have a big education seminar with speakers coming in to promote their congregation.

These are expenses that they did not have to incur, but they did so because they had the money to make it possible.

One can then make the argument in a credit presentation that these discretionary items could be added back to cash flow. This same concept can be used with regular businesses as well if you can demonstrate that the item is non-recurring or something that you only did because you had the extra cash to do it.

It may seem that I am getting a little into the weeds, but that is a lot of what I do in my business. I help companies tell their business story in a way that makes financial sense to a lender and credit analyst.

Chapter 21

Most Overlooked Items

"There is no harm in hoping for the best as long as you're prepared for the worst." Stephen King

AR Aging, AP Aging, Inventory List, Top 10 Customers

The above line alone is a lot to unpack, and many of these may not apply to your business. If they do not, feel free to move on to the next item.

AR Aging report

This is important because it shows how well you are handling your collections and if you have a concentration on certain accounts. Any client that makes up more than 20% of your balances or total business in a year is considered a concentration risk. If you lose that one account, it can dramatically impact your company.

Remember this; your best client is someone else's best prospect. In business, we know there is ALWAYS a Risk of losing accounts. I hear the defeated voices from business owners all the time with lines of, "But Bill, we have done business with them for years. They are our top client, blah blah blah." Yeah, I get it, but there is still a financial risk to a lender here, and it needs to be discussed and addressed. Some financing sources will focus on the quality of your AR And clients more than your business strength.

You need to have an action plan explaining the various ways you plan on widening your client base to reduce dependence on anyone's account. If you are applying for some type of working capital line of credit that will be monitored with a borrowing base, do not be surprised if there is an exclusion for account balances over a certain threshold (usually 20-25%). The Age of your accounts is also a factor. If you have large balances over 60-90 days past due, this is another red flag, ESPECIALLY if they are with your largest clients.

I have seen this time and time again. I have even heard the "We give our best clients flexibility in paying us back because we don't want to lose them." Look, I understand business is a balancing act, and you are simply trying to keep your clients and other things rolling. Just understand that this is a perceived risk from a lender and needs to be discussed. IMPORTANT NOTE: If you are offering terms other than net 30 to any of your clients, you need to let the lender know. Most accounting software will assume that the terms are net 30.

If you are allowing the client to pay Net 45 or Net 60, the account will look past due even though it is not. I have seen this several times, so be prepared to explain the terms that are beyond net 30. I am in no way trying to tell you how to run your business but hoping to make you aware that they need to understand if you are doing anything unusual.

I have been fortunate to help clients negotiate fair deals on their lines of credit. Having the information available to help the bank make a straightforward decision made the process smoother. Remember that uncertainty and questions are flags that might lead to risk in the mind of a lender. If the answer is not clear, they will assume the worst-case scenario.

Accounts Payable

Again, the lender is making judgments of the age of your receivables and dependence on a small number of suppliers. Payables that are over 60-90 days past due are a big red flag to a bank. They assume that you are having liquidity problems and having trouble paying your bills. Some borrowers will snap at me here and say, "If I could pay all my bills, I wouldn't need a loan."

Fair warning- DO NOT ever say that to a bank, but you CAN say that to me as your consultant. I can help you find a way to explain the working capital situation. Also, if you are too dependent on a small number of suppliers, a bank may want to know you have alternated in case something happens with your primary.

Inventory

If you manufacture a product, chances are you have raw material, Work In Process (WIP), and finished goods. Other businesses like retailers and distributors might only have finished goods. I also understand that some of the businesses I work with do not have an inventory component at all. But if you do, the lender will try and understand what you have and if any of it is old, and how it could affect the loan.

Top 10 Client list

This is not necessarily required and is not on most checklists, but I have found it is vital information to have. It comes in especially handy if you are dealing with some impressive clients and have new business to do with them soon. It is also helpful if your historical cash flow is weak but your company is growing. If you have contracts and orders in the process of being filled or will be filling, it will add the strength of your cash flow projections. These usually are not conventional bank sources, but I have access to them as an alternative.

Business Debt Schedule

This is one of the most important items that is commonly left off or incomplete. The unfortunate thing is that this is very simple and easy to provide that would make such a difference. Here is a link to some free resources we offer our clients, including a debt schedule https://www.NoBullShitBusinessFinanceGuide.com/No-BS-Free-Resources/

This schedule will be dated the same as your Interim Financial Statements. So, if you have a balance sheet say- Month End August 31st of the current year, you will date the debt schedule with the same date, and the balances need to match the liabilities in that statement. Can you get away with a debt schedule that does not tie into your most recent financial statement? Yes, BUT it might get sent back.

Chapter 22

Keep the Analyst Happy

"I'll often joke that when people ask, 'What is a business analyst?' I say: You know all those times people say 'Somebody should look into that?' I'm the person who looks into that." Jen Neuls

Keeping the Analyst happy

Again, everything you do or do not is building credibility with the Credit Analyst. You might bring a tear to his eye when he sees that the statements match up. No, really it is a huge deal to them and might even make them feel better about your loan. As an easier alternative, if you brought me in as your consultant, I would work with you and your accounting staff on putting all this together.

In addition to the balances, you will need to have the original balance of the loans, date they were originated, maturity date, monthly payments, current balance (as of the most recent month end), and interest rate.

You might be asking, "Why do they need all of that information?" Simply put, they are going to use this to calculate your cash required to service debt in addition to the loan payment for the new loan you are requesting. If we do not give them a clear answer of what the payments are, THEY WILL ASSUME THE WORST.

I am not being critical of the credit analyst here. Their job is to be cautious and protect the banks interest. If they must "assume" something, they are going to be conservative in those assumptions. For example, if you had an equipment loan on a seven-year amortization with a low payment, they might assume it has to be paid over three years. If you have another piece of real estate with a loan amortized over 20 years, they might predict 15 if you do not tell them.

The same goes if someone has a great rate of 2.99%, but if they are not told of a payment or an interest rate, they might hike it up to 10%. It has happened, and it is a hassle, and we might find ourselves back to square one.

By providing clear information, companies are helping their chances of getting the best treatment in the cash flow calculation. We do not have to like it. But by helping you understand what you are up against, these little details are like gold to the person you are preparing this file for. What we like does not matter because they are the ones writing the check.

Bait the Hook

I know that sounds harsh but think about it. When you are selling a product or service, are you more interested in what your client needs or what you want? As anglers say in fishing, "You need to bait they hook to suit the fish." I get it, business owners are super busy running their company, and they want to get these stupid checklists done as soon as possible.

When I work with a client, I will identity someone internally at their company that is my real go to person for completing the package. Sometimes it is the Office Manager, the Accountant, Controller, etc.

It is usually someone that helps keep all the back-office things running while the entrepreneur is out hustling for business.

What I believe has helped make our business successful is that I understand business owners, and I understand what banks are looking for. Acting as a guide and mediator will allow you to vent and bitch about how stupid all these things are that we ask for. Hopefully, without the bank having to hear it, so we are not thrown back in the lake. I will calmly listen, tell you to suck it up (if you want), and get me what we need so I can keep fishing.

SCHEDULE OF COLLATERAL(A quick breakdown)

If you are buying real estate, business equipment, or even something tangible with the loan proceeds, you will need to provide some details about that here. I suggest you also provide supporting information in the packet that will help the analyst understand the collateral and its value. In real estate, you might have the marketing PDF included with the listing or with equipment. You might even have details from their sales brochures.

In this section, we are painting a picture for the analyst of what you are purchasing, how it will help your business, and how valuable it is. If you have existing business assets that have not been included on your debt schedule referenced above, also include that here. Here is a link to some free resources we offer our clients, including a schedule of collateral at
https://www.NoBullShitBusinessFinanceGuide.com/No-BS-Free-Resources/

Collateral is what is your bank calls your "Secondary source of repayment." When the bank considers your loan, the value, and marketability of the proposed collateral will affect the loan terms. As a rule, the more specialized the collateral, the less valuable it to the bank. Which is why if you are buying a special use property like a hotel, restaurant, car wash, mini storage facility, etc., you have a harder time finding financing.

In other cases, the lender will have a lower Loan-To-Value (LTV) threshold. In this case, they are factoring in concerns with having a limited market to sell the asset to if they must take it back from you. There is a lot more detail about this in my section on the 5 C's of credit.

Your Company

The bank needs to get a sense of your company. You would be surprised how hard it is for some people to explain this. Consider using some of your sales material here. Really try to sell the reader on why they would want to do business with you.

Think about it. You are asking a lender to put up two to four times as much cash than you to benefit your project. For those of you bothered by my math, I am estimating LTV's of 65-80% at 65 they are putting up two to one, and at 80 percent, it is four to one that the lender is putting in for each dollar of equity you are contributing.

The point is, why would you not try and "sell" the lender on the strengths of your business? I am not talking about going overboard, but just some basic info. They need to get a feel of who you are and why you are good at what you do.

Management Team/Ownership Resumes

This goes hand in hand with the Company section listed above. What makes you and your team special? If this was an SBA loan, a resume/bio on each owner would be a requirement. Conventional loans do not necessarily ask for this, but I believe it helps to reader understand your business.

This is where we transition from the Personal information requested. I get a lot of borrowers that ask me for "Non- Recourse" financing and then ask why we have to request their personal information as part of the loan package. Remember, the area I am focusing on with this book privately helps businesses with annual sales anywhere between $500,000 and $50 Million. Whether we like it or not, understanding your personal financials is a critical part of considering financing for businesses in this space. Even if the lender considers a non-recourse or limited recourse option, they need to feel confident that you have a strong personal financial footing and will not be a drain on the business. As I have stated several times, I am not asking you to like it; I am just helping you navigate the way things are.

Complete Personal Tax returns (With K-1's from any business returns that feed into your personal)

I am certain I just got a cheer from all the credit analysts reading this section. Yes, the lender is going to ask for three years of your complete personal tax returns. If you have other entities that feed into it, they will likely ask for those too. *"But Bill, I don't want my other companies to have to sign on this loan!"* That is okay.

At this stage, the analyst is simply getting a feel of your complete financial picture. The lender, on the other hand, is trying to size up the personal returns of the owners. They are asking themselves questions like, "Are these clients a drain or an asset to the business? Have they created a lifestyle where they HAVE TO take out $250,000 per year regardless of how good or bad the company is doing? Will they have income from other outside sources that could help the business if they fall on hard times?" We will cover this more in the PFS section. If you succeed, then they know the bank is safe as well. They must consider everything.

Chapter 23

Grade Yourself – What If You Don't Fit the Credit Box

"You never find yourself until you face the truth." Pearl Bailey

Are You Bankable - Grade Yourself

Now that you have seen the 5 C's of Credit and a typical loan package for the type of deal you are requesting, how do you score on the 5 C's? I would encourage you to evaluate yourself in each area to be prepared for what type of questions you will get from the bank.

Here is a link to some free resources we offer our clients, including a Self-Evaluation Sheet at

https://www.NoBullShitBusinessFinanceGuide.com/No-BS-Free-Resources/.

Scoring well on the sheet is not going to guarantee success in your financing, but it will give you a good idea of what you will be up against.

Based on the answers to your questions, rank yourself on a scale of 1-5 in each category (1 Being weak and 5 being Very Strong)

1. Character

A. How does your business look in this area?
B. Can you clearly articulate the history of your company, reputation in the market?

C. How is your personal credit? If you have any issues with your credit, be ready to explain and document what happened.
D. How about the D & B or Paydex on your business? (we can pull these for you as part of our process)

2. Capacity to Repay *Remember, HISTORICAL TAX RETURNS Are what matter for regular bank loans.*

A. Has your business been profitable for the last 3 years?
B. Are the trends positive or negative, or sporadic?
C. Is your Cash available to service debt/EBITDA sufficient to cover your payments? <u>Most banks want at least a 1.25 Time Debt Service Coverage, sometimes higher depending on your industry or project type.</u>

3. Capital Both Business and Personal

A. How highly leveraged are you right now, and how highly leveraged will you be after the loan?
B. How liquid are you/your company?
C. If you look at your current assets compared to current liabilities (quick ratio), are you at risk of running out of money for your short-term obligations?

4. Collateral

A. What is the collateral being pledged for the request?
B. If you are buying real estate, equipment, etc., how much are you contributing in comparison to how much you are asking to be financed? *Remember depending on the collateral type; a different down payment expectation will be required. As a general rule, other than some cases in equipment finance, most lenders expect you to have some "skin in the game."*

5. Conditions (it is good to be ready with answers

A. How is the overall US economy right now?
B. How is the local economy where you will be doing business?

C. How is the industry you are in (growing or contracting)?
D. What is your position within the industry? *Just keep in mind that these are things the lending source will think about.*
E. How strong or weak is your management team and succession planning?
F. Financing Source you are working with - Is your industry, project type and credit profile in line with their credit appetite?

For a sample worksheet to grade your business, go to https://www.NoBullShitBusinessFinanceGuide.com/No-BS-Free-Resources/

Scoring

<u>Scores of 20-25</u> It sounds like you check all the boxes, and obtaining conventional financing shouldn't be too hard. For you, we will be helping you get the best pricing terms and turnaround time. (Again, we can't "guarantee" anything, but if your answers check out, you should have some options)

<u>Score 15-20</u> OK in this range. You are borderline but may have some good mitigating circumstances. It will take a little more work to find the right lending source for you. Conventional financing may be available, but we may be looking at alternative sources that we will cover in detail in the next chapter (Book).

<u>Score 10-15</u> If you score in this range, you may have already been turned down at a few banks and may already be frustrated with the process. There might be a story here that allows us to help you find alternate financing, but you definitely could benefit from professional help. One challenge you might have in this range is coming to grips with the perceived risk of your request compared to the pricing and terms you expect.

<u>Score below 10</u> You may not be finance-able at all. You may need to bring in an equity partner or guarantor to strengthen the overall file. Depending on the type of financing you are requesting, we

might be able to find you a specialty lender that can look past some of your challenges if there are offsetting strengths. Again, all of these are case by case.

Scores between 1 and 5 5- You are well above expectations in this category. 3- Right at the limit 2- Below, but you have a good story of why it is low and how you are going to make it better. 1 Well below.

What are my options

Regardless of how well or low you scored yourself in the previous section, there could be some options out there for you. It all depends on what you are trying to accomplish. In the next section/book I will go into detail on some of the different financing options available out there. Again, this book is geared towards privately held companies that are not looking to sell equity in their business. As a rule, debt financing is considered the least expensive cost of capital when you take into consideration the opportunity cost and control you may give it, bringing in equity capital. I have nothing against equity, but that is not what this book is about.

If you are looking for Crowdfunding, Private equity deals, Shark Tank, or whatever, you are not going to find that in this book. If you really want me to write about that, I can; just shoot me an email at bill@4kingscapital.com. If there is enough interest, I would be happy to explain all that stuff. The point is, do not give up hope. There are other options out there for your business.

Chapter 24

Introduction to Non- Bank Lenders

"Tough times never last, but tough people do." Robert H. Schuller

What exactly is a non-bank lender?

Years ago, when I first got started in banking, I was a member of a commercial real estate networking group. I remember always seeing a big burly guy that was always at these meetings. To protect the innocent, we will call him Bruno.

This guy was what I call a knuckle and kneecaps hard money lender. You do not try to miss a payment with these types of guys. They are still around today and are very much a part of the "Hard Money" portion of the market, but they are only a small part of it.

In the private lending space, you have financing sources that can get a better return on their money by lending it out to business owners and investors on deals traditional banks cannot do. They will still look carefully at the 5 C's of credit (outlined in the first section), but they generally have a higher risk tolerance.

Typically, in a non-bank transaction, there is a particular strength in the deal they really like. This in turn, allows them to work around the other weaknesses. These loans are more expensive and are intended as a "Bridge to Bankable." These lenders know you are not going to be their client long-term and price it accordingly. One of my strengths as a consultant is to help clients transition from regular bank financing after a couple of years with a nontraditional source.

OVERVIEW OF FINANCING OPTIONS

I thought all financing is the same? No, no it is not.

There are a lot of people in my industry that over-promise and under deliver. I wish there was an easier option, but the truth is, "THERE IS NO EASY BUTTON" in business financing. You can find countless advertisements out there of brokers promising "Low Interest," "Unsecured," "Quick Turnaround," and other buzzwords they throw out there. They want to catch the entrepreneur with the unrealistic promise of what they want to hear. Unfortunately for the client, it was a laboring process where they found themselves repeatedly starting because of that deceptive Over Promise.

I never promise what I know is unrealistic to deliver, and honestly, I know I have lost a lot of deals because of it. At the same time, I have clients coming back after taking a beating. They later realized that what I told them was true.

I will never reopen a deal with the undertones of "I told you so." I would hate that if I were sitting at the other end of the desk. I know how tough it is out there, and I respect entrepreneurs too much to be that asshole. We will just pick up where we left off and work to get the deal done. Your business deserves that.

Many of my clients will tell you I am brutally honest. Am I always right? Of course not. No one is perfect, but with 20 years under my belt, I get close to the mark.

When I look at a credit file, using what the wife refers to as my "Spidy senses,"- I size it up and find the category it will most likely go into. My mind races to which lending sources fit in with that deal. If I have learned anything about lending sources is that they are all different and require various things that fit in their box. I then consider what our best options are within that category.

What most of my competitors have done and do is throw out the best option that might be available and sell you on that. Once they already have you committed to them, more times than not, it is discovered that you are not going to qualify for what you thought you were getting. Then you find yourself back at square one after time lost with more built-up frustration.

Here is an outline of different types of financing options that I typically encounter and what types of situations they are appropriate for. Fortunately for us, we offer various types of financing if your deal is not "bankable" with a traditional lender.

Even within the traditional lender world, there are variations depending on the type of bank and their credit appetite. This list is not going to be exhaustive, but I will explain the various types out there. You deserve to know what works for your business, and I am not going to bullshit you on what to expect.

A good example of using various nonbank options would be my client XYZ Skin Care in the cosmetics business(yes, I made that name up to protect the innocent, but the story is real). The client was referred to me after having been turned down at maybe nine or ten banks for their expansion.

I will never forget my first meeting with one of the owners. After learning about their business and touring the facility, we sat back down, and he said, "By the way, in addition to the $2 Million expansion loan, I need $500,000 by next week for an order we have to pay off, or we lose a big client". I honestly thought this must be a joke and almost fell out of my chair. He was completely serious, so my brain got to work. How can I structure this, who can I send him to etc. The pressure was on.

This was going to be a classic SBA International trade deal (you will learn more about that in the next chapter). I was confident I could find a non-bank SBA lender that would do this deal, but there is no way it will fund in a week. Now what I needed was a short-term deal lender.

I got to work, and after talking to dozens of sources, I found one of my more aggressive factoring lenders. They were not only able to provide the client the $500,000 they needed but also additional working capital while we worked on the SBA loan to refinance the short-term loan and complete their expansion.

It was a huge challenge, but one where I needed complete honesty and responsiveness from the client to make it happen. It was a great case of using a few different out of the box resources. The borrower would never have found the answers on their own, even though they had worked hard talking to different banks. They were about to give up hope when we were able to step in and help with their obstacles. We continue to hear from them and wish them the best of luck.

Chapter 25

Alternate Financing Sources

"Just the facts Ma'am." -Joe Friday Dragnet

The short answers if you do not fit into the Credit Box

SBA Financing

SBA lending is probably one of the most misunderstood financing options out there for small business owners. Think of SBA financing as an expansion of each individual lender's credit box. The reason a lender will be more flexible in using an SBA loan is that a portion of their risk is guaranteed by the Small Business Administration. The lender in essence, is receiving an insurance policy on the financing they are provided. This does not mitigate all of their risks, but it does lower the potential losses. By doing so, then allows the lender can be more flexible.

Another advantage of SBA financing for the borrower is that you can (typically) have a lower down payment and a longer amortization on the loan than would be allowed in traditional bank financing. SBA financing is an entire training on its own, so I am just touching on it briefly here. In the following chapters, I go on to explain more in-depth what SBA is and the different segments in it.

Purchase Order Financing

This type of financing is typically used when a small business lands a large contract that will strain their business financially and need extras to fulfill the new requirement. They may need new equipment, additional employees, working capital, or a variety of other things.

This financing is also focused more on the quality of the client the borrower is partnering with than the financial strength of the borrower themselves. The major difference between Purchase Order Financing and Factoring is that a PO financier is lending against the value of the contract.

The borrower's contract still has to perform where a factoring service has a tangible Account Receivable that are due to the borrower for products/services already delivered. PO Financing is generally very expensive and is often provided by the same lender that will provide factoring of the A/R.

Factoring Services

A Factoring lender is, in essence, buying the rights to the accounts receivable due to the borrower. They are focused more on borrowers' client's quality and typically only accept business receivables. If the small business deals with reputable companies and has strong performance, they might qualify for this type of financing. Pricing and structure range widely depending on various factors. This has become a great option for various clients for revolving capital.

Non-Bank Equipment Financing

Lenders in the Equipment Finance Space are focused more on the quality of the Equipment being purchased or leased than the quality of the borrower. There is a wide range of sources in this space, from A to D credits and some that will even finance startups. Again, the pricing varies with the risk and the quality of the equipment being purchased. Normally, these lenders will finance up to 100% of the Purchase price, plus some soft costs. Regrettably, the cost of funds is generally higher than bank financing.

Merchant Cash Advance

Rant: I do not like this kind of financing but am mentioning it to let my audience know that it exists. There are multiple variations of this type of financing. They are more focused on your average sales per month, particularly your average credit card receipts.

This type of financing has a tendency of being very expensive and is a difficult cycle to get out of. Once you get into it, getting out can be tough. The marketing strategy of lenders in this space is that their application process is generally easy compared to other sources, and they can fund very quickly, but it comes at a price.

Private Money/Hard Money CRE – Bridge Financing

I have combined these two because the only major difference is pricing and advance rate between the two. This financing looks primarily at the quality/type of Real Estate project first, and everything else becomes secondarily. Private money is more competitive in pricing and structure but also has higher underwriting standards.

More Often Than Not, private money lenders will focus on a few asset classes that they are comfortable with. Hard Money financing generally requires a larger down payment from the borrower, has higher price and fees, but is not as concerned with the other aspects of the borrower's eligibility like Credit Score, Cashflow, Experience, etc.).

I am fortunate to work with lenders in these spaces that are credible and that I trust. If working directly with myself, I will look over the package and see what options work best for your needs. This is a hard world to navigate for most people if they are going at it alone. My hope is to help prepare you for what to expect.

Chapter 26

SBASimplified- The Banker and the Bookie

"At the end of the day, they are really betting on the management team's ability to execute the business plan." Don Carson

Betting on your business

With the hit of COVID causing an introduction to PPP loans, SBA financing has received a lot more publicity. There is a great deal of information and even more misinformation out there about what SBA is and what it is not. I could have easily included SBA in the previous sections since these types of loans are available through both bank and non-bank lenders, but I felt that it was complicated enough that it deserved a section of its own.

Depending on demand, I might write a book just about SBA financing. Again, if you are interested in that, send me a message at bill@billwritethisbook.com

The way I ended up being the go-to SBA guy was that I understood credit surprisingly well and was always trying to look for different ways to get deals done. In my banking career, I have done more SBA loans than I can remember.

One of my roles was managing an entire SBA team. Did I want to be "An SBA Guy"? No, as a matter of fact, most of my colleagues can agree that we did not plan on going into the exciting world of SBA lending.

Having been a credit decision-maker in several of the roles over the years, I understood the risk banks were looking at. I also learned that as a bank executive, the powers that be do not have much patience for mistakes. Fortunately, I have been involved in handling hundreds of millions of dollars in financing over the years. But the deals I cannot forget the most are the ones that went bad.

In that dark place is where the uncomfortable truth dwells and a place we as lenders never want to be in. I bet that is true for most commercial lenders out there. With that said, there are times that you really want to do a loan, but it just does not meet your credit policy; that is where SBA comes in.

The Gambler

When I speak to groups, one of the examples I use is this- Think of banking as betting on a business because that is what lenders do. They are betting that your business will succeed, and you will be able to pay them back. Their return on that bet is the interest they make on loan.

In an abstract way, lenders are really gamblers. Insert the Kenny Rogers music now. In this case, the banker/gambler looks at a million-dollar loan and decides, "You know what, this is just a little too risky for us; come back in a few years."

Now a new character emerges that works with the gambler. The Bookie (SBA guy) is the player who accepts and pays off the bets. My SBA people do not kill me for this one. I am making a point. The bookie comes up and tells the banker/gambler, "Hey, I will make you a deal. I like this business owner's deal, and it meets all our requirements. For a small fee, I will give you three to one odds on your deal."

"What do you mean?" the banker asks.

"Well, we will guarantee this loan for the borrower, and if it goes south, we will pay you 75% of your losses."

The banker/gambler scratches his chin, considering the deal. "That is something to think about. Maybe I can get there on those terms...". That is the gist of how this type of SBA financing works.

Now for all of my banker friends out there losing their minds, I know it is not quite this simplistic, but it does explain what an SBA 7A loan, in essence, does. I know you need to document your file the right way and that SBA will check the file closely if you ever make a claim, which is why lenders must be very picky when they are doing these deals.

I am going to give you more details about some of the different SBA programs in the next section and where you would commonly see them. Again, this list may not be all-inclusive and subject to change. To look up current information on SBA loans, go to www.SBA.gov.

What I am showing you here are some tips based on my experience, and I am not claiming to work for the SBA or to be able to guarantee anyone's success in getting a loan approved. Yes, the blood-sucking lawyers made me say that.

Chapter 27

Most common SBA Programs

"A bank is a place where they lend you an umbrella in fair weather and ask for it back when it begins to rain." Robert Frost

SBA 7A

The most used SBA program is under the Flagship 7A Umbrella. Depending on which source you are dealing with, you can borrow from as little as $25,000 and up to about $5 Million. There are some exceptions here, but that is the general range.

As I mentioned in the previous section, this type of SBA loan is, in essence, a guarantee that if you screw up and cannot pay the loan back, the SBA will step in and pay some of the losses for the bank.

You might be thinking, "*Why do I care if they help the blood-sucking bank out when I am the one going bankrupt?*" That is a good point, but keep in mind that you probably would not have even been able to get financing at the terms you would be getting without an SBA guarantee.

They are betting on you, but in all fairness, they need to protect themselves from taking the risk. Most companies generally need to obtain this type of loan for one of two reasons:

1. They cannot get approved without some type of enhancement. If you go back to the chapter on the 5 C's of credit and Scoring the Business part, chances are they may have been weak in at least one to two areas. If there is weakness in three or more, there is a higher probability it will get turned down, even with an SBA guarantee. In a case like

that, there might be other options depending on the situation. I will discuss those more in another chapter.

2. They could get approved for a conventional loan but really want to put less money down, want a longer amortization, some combination of these, or other factors. In other words, they can get approved but not on the terms they would like. Sometimes it is as simple as that.

One of the things that I remind my clients is Cashflow is King (pun intended). For small business owners, whether you are growing or facing a rough patch, your ability to pay your bills and maintain your liquidity is the most important thing. This will be true for most businesses up to about $10-15 Million in sales. Even though the problem has not gone away, remember that the dynamics are simply changing.

SBA 504

Another Capital option for Real Estate deals

Let us say you are buying a building and you want to get the lowest down payment, longest amortization, and a low-interest rate. Ideally, that is what we all want. One option, assuming you qualify, is to do an SBA 504 loan. One thing I have noticed about fellow bankers is we all love Real Estate and fixed asset deals. The joke being, "We love it as long as they are 'Cash Flow Lenders' and the client has collateral."

My banker friends know I give them a hard time about this. Maybe our humor is not for everyone. The truth is, A 504 loan can only be used in transactions related to owner-occupied commercial real estate, heavy equipment purchases, and in some cases refinancing these asset types.

The nuances of the program constantly change, so please go to SBA.gov to double-check if there are any changes since the writing of this book. This loan type can be problematic, and I recommend professional supervision if you are going to try one of these. But for the sake of argument, I will give you a quick explanation of how they work.

If you had a machine shop and have been leasing your building for several years and now the owner wants to sell it to you for $2 Million. You apply for a conventional loan and will likely need to put 20-25% down, and the amortization will be 15-20 years, depending on the age, condition and type of building you are buying. Yes, I know you can get 25 years conventional on some deals, but that is not as common as most may think.

After the building purchase, you decide to make renovations but did not in the past because you were only leasing. With the renovations, $500,000 is now tacked on. Now your project total is now $2.5 Million, and you find yourself needing to come up with $500,000 cash to make this happen. That is a big chunk of change for anyone running a business. One option for this scenario would be to consider a 504 loan.

You can get away with as little as 10% down and an amortization of 25 years, while some lenders may even be able to do 30 on the first lien. Remember, a "Lien" is the legal right or claim against the property by the creditor. It is the ability to keep possessions of property etc., belonging to another person until that debt owned by that person is discharged. Here are the nuts and bolts of this type of deal in a 504 structure. You will put your $250,000 into the project, and the bank/lender will do an interim construction loan for the remaining $2,250,000.

During the approval process, you may be introduced to a Certified Development Company (CDC). They are normally nonprofits that take care of the SBA portion of these loans and are licensed in each state.

The CDC varies depending on each state. Here in Texas, the CDC will not typically be the same one in Arkansas, New York, or wherever. The good news is they do serve the same function. What they will do is buy out up to 40% of the project from the bank loan and be inserted in the 2nd lien.

This loan is 100% guaranteed by the SBA and is typically sold to investors in the secondary market. It is called a Debenture, and the rates are usually very low compared to the prevailing interest rate. November 2020, as I am writing this, it is below 3% and FIXED FOR

THE ENTIRE 25 Years, so it may change by the time you are reading this book.

The bank is now in the first lien position, and they will only have 50% risk on the project. This makes us bankers feel warm and fuzzy to have a commercial real estate loan with a low loan to value. This type of example is great because it is very common in 504 deals and could easily be a manufacturer, service company or any other type of business.

I personally try to avoid special use properties and start ups because they are far more complicated and even harder to explain. If you do run into one of those scenarios, expect that you will have to put 15-20% down, but you still get the lower rate and longer amortization.

Chapter 28

SBA International Trade Program – Best Kept Secret

"I feel I've got unfinished business at an international level." Brian
Ashton

International Trade

I am constantly amazed that this program is not used more. Let us go back to the analogy of the SBA being a bookie and giving the blood-sucking lender three to one odds on their deal. I had a client not long ago in the consumer electronics business that sold their products here in the States, Canada and other parts of the world.

They desperately needed permanent working capital for their growing business. When I use the term "permanent working capital." I am talking about the capital needed to run the business that is not expected to cycle in 60-90 days like regular working capital. Now I will take that to a whole new level. Let us say that your business sells internationally. I realize there are other ways to qualify for this program but let me keep it simple as I stick with a basic exporter example.

Now I know there are some out there that love to knit; pick me on this, but for the sake of explaining it to the novice learner, let us not go there. Side note: If we ever have a drink, I would be happy to tell you about this jerk at a little community bank that tried to "correct me" on this point in front of a client.

First in business, do not ever do this to anyone, including myself. Trying to show your dominance makes people you are working with look dumb is never received well. I felt a need to kindly put him in his place then and there. I thought I used tact; my wife disagreed but not before telling me the "ass deserved it."

Word to young bankers out there, some of us old guys have fought some intense battles, are cranky, and no longer care about being politically correct. Then again, maybe that is just me. He did not get the deal or any referrals.

Back to the international deal. This one was about $2.1 million. Well, if the business qualified for the international trade program, the SBA would give the bank an incentive with up to a 90% guarantee on their loan. For those of you that are not math geeks or of a bookie mindset like me, that is a nine to one odds on your money. It appears to be a safe bet, but they STILL have to underwrite the risk. All the bases must be covered. If the SBA found a lender was out there gunslinging 90% guarantee deals like they were candy, they would shut that down quick.

I have seen that ugly scenario happen so many times. I get borrowers all the time that proclaim, "Well, if the SBA is guaranteeing it, why do they not just approve all of the loans?" Quickest answer- Because there is no guarantee, they will receive the guarantee.

SBA is constantly updating and changing their programs, but the overall goal of providing financing to small businesses when they are having trouble obtaining conventional financing will always remain a part of their mission. For additional information about the programs I have outlined in this chapter, and for more details about other resources that are available to you, please go to www.SBA.Gov

Chapter 29

USDA - Small and Rural Communities

"There's a lot more business out there in small town America than I ever dreamed of." -Sam Walton

USDA B &I

In full disclosure, I have not done a lot of these, but I felt I should let my readers know they are out there. These types of loans are like SBA in that the government is providing the lender a guarantee. Doing so it would help to encourage them to make loans that they otherwise would not.

The biggest difference between these types of loans and SBA is that they are intended to encourage investment in Rural markets. As a general rule, they are mostly available in communities with a population less than 50,000 people that are not part of a metropolitan area.

For example, I live out in the Dallas Fort Worth area. If someone wanted to apply for a B & I loan for a smaller town near us like the city of Parker. While Parker has less than 50,000 people, it would not qualify because it is part of the DFW (Dallas Fort Worth)- MSA.

I do not make the rules, but that is how this system works. On the other hand, let us say that someone wanted to build a project in the tiny town of Duncan, Oklahoma (where my wife grew up). That should qualify.

As of the writing of this book, the population of Duncan is less than 25,000 and nowhere near or part or even a suburb of a big city. It has a complete small-town vibe with almost one of everything.

That kind of place might work. To confirm if a project is eligible, reference the USDA map at

https://eligibility.sc.egov.usda.gov/eligibility/welcomeAction.do

Another advantage of B & I deals is that the USDA does not care how big the business is, that requesting the loan serving as an advantage in this space. While in the SBA world, financing is limited to small companies as defined by the SBA. The mission of the SBA is to help Small Businesses grow in their current markets.

The Mission of the USDA B & I Program is to promote growth in rural markets, and they are more lenient with who does it. Let us not get ahead of ourselves, you cannot get a B & I loan on a strip club or a casino- I am talking about the size of the business borrower. If a big company wanted to build a shopping center in a rural town, they could use this type of program to do that and have a better chance of qualifying for this type of loan. If you are interested in learning more, reach out to Business & Industry Loan Guarantees | Rural Development (usda.gov)

Chapter 30

Kick in the Teeth

"You may not realize it when it happens, but a kick in the teeth may be the best thing that ever happens to you." Walt Disney

Get your Ass Back Up

I got the $Hit kicked out of me by corporate America for the last time before going out on my own. Now, like most of you, I know the humiliation of working for an organization only to have them turn their back on you. This is a difficult thing for me to bring up, but I write about it to remind you that not everyone will see your worth. How you respond when you need to get back up speaks more of your character than those trying to knock you down.

This was the last straw of getting knocked down for me. The bank I worked for unexpectedly demoted me on the spot. They then had the audacity to introduce me to my replacement five minutes later. I was expected to stay, train him, hand him my growing portfolio, introduce him to the team I had single handedly staffed, but do it with a smile on my face as if I knew this was coming.

A few weeks before this incident, I had organized an entire meet and greeted launch with over a hundred people that included the out-of-town bosses. They were the same ones now telling me of this new magical candidate that came highly recommended from an outside source.

Much to their surprise, I refused to introduce him to my team that day. I knew my staff would not take it well, and I was right. To add more treachery to an already tarnished moment, I found out weeks later that they left the Meet and Greeted early to interview him.

Unbeknownst to me, I was left entertaining our guests while they snuck away. I also discovered my replacement was later bragging about the incident. It only demonstrated to me and others the quality of man they had chosen. These were not the respectable partners I had once deemed worthy. To say I was blindside was an understatement.

I felt defeated and so damn angry. I had worked so hard, sacrificing my family and even my health just to have it all crash down on me. Unable to wrap my head around the betrayal, I chose to leave early that day and phoned someone I knew had my corner no matter where I ended up. I called The Wife. "Come home," is all I remember her saying from the limbo of my thoughts.

She greeted me in the kitchen with open arms, and we stood holding each other in silence. Her voice is usually so sweet, but, at this moment, it held a hint of anger and assurance.

She then said the words I never expected to hear from her. "Honey, we are now officially done with banking. It is time." She looked me square in the eyes and said, "You have been preparing for this, and the time has come for you to go out on your own. Never again will the small-minded opinions of weak men control your life."

She then kindly reminded me of all the things I had accomplished in my 20-year career. She listed the various awards I had won and even the unrealistic objectives each bank had set that I reached. Most importantly, she ingrained in me the countless people I had helped.

"YOU did that Bill. Your genius, drive and work ethic have always been unstoppable. They let you go because they were fools who refused to see it. Be proud of what you ALONE have accomplished..."

She was wrong about one big thing. I had not done it alone. She always had there. She was always ready to lend an ear, praying over me, telling me the hard truths, and most importantly, being a soft place for this hard-ass man.

I decided that I had no other choice but to get back up. I worked my ass off and in six months managed to earn what would have taken me a year working for at that bank.

Going out on my own was the best decision I ever made. I believe my business will continue to succeed because I refuse to stay defeated. My faith and being a good woman have kept me standing. Knowing that I can help other business owners who have been knocked down, well, that keeps me going.

Carefully choosing strong, honest lenders and referral sources that also want to help these people has been such a great honor. I know together, we can make a difference. These days I am lucky to work with people like that.

Help is Here

With the mental anguish I managed to describe in the above paragraphs, I almost titled this section "You Might Need Professional Help." I am certain some of you may have remembered a moment like that where you too were knocked on your ass with hope almost lost. And yet, you are still standing.

As a business owner, I am sure you had family members and friends call you crazy. Perhaps they even questioned to your face how they would never leave the security of a job because of that steady paycheck.

I too, heard the defeating words from family and friends in the past like, "He should get a real job. Look at all the money you could lose. Bill, you'll never make it. Etc.". Later in life, it was, "He's crazy to leave a six-figure job!" It was enough to drive a man crazy or even quit, but it is not who we are.

The "professional help" I am talking about is not mental, but what you are doing for your business. It is about seeking qualified support with putting together your finance packages, learning to obtain capital to run those businesses. Now many clients have CPA's, Attorney, or even In House Accountants, and that is great. The only obstacle to that is they, unfortunately, are not in market EVERY day looking for finance sources. I am.

They have their hands full, managing other things for the business. When I come into the picture, it becomes a partnership as we both work together to help the client. You are great at what you do, so I ask: Why not let someone help with the finance part?

Chapter 31

Three Types of Clients We Help

"The man sent a bill that read -Tapping with the hammer $2.
Knowing where to tap $9,998."

Three Categories of Clients

1)Story Credit Client

These clients are having trouble finding financing. They may be weak in a few of the 5'cs, have been turned down at a bank already, or have a complicated deal. They need help because they are not getting approved. The scenarios could be having wrong lending sources, deal structured wrong, etc.

2)Need for Speed Client

Now, these customers have a time crunch. There is an urgency to get a loan. They typically already have good financial strength but might need to purchase equipment, real estate or just upgrade to accommodate a big purchase order. Their need is speed.

3)Wake up the Bankers Client

These clients are a growing part of my field. These companies have a good business. They are wonderful at what they do, have strong financials, and are looking to grow. They need a substantial loan and see the value of having a specialist like myself. I help find lending sources, but If we work with the existing bank, we find their banks suddenly being more accommodating. They want to keep the client and become more flexible.

If you as a client have a great relationship with your bank, GOOD! We do not want to give you the added hassle of moving over the entire relationship as we work on your deals. We know that there are some great bankers out there that truly value their customers, and we are in no way wanting to come between that. I am more than happy to work with them, and we usually form a nice team to help find the best deals for the clients.

Bankers, too, become frustrated with deals their bank cannot do. They do not want to tell the customers "No," but sometimes their hands are tied. What I can usually do is find local or out of town lenders specifically for the project.

It becomes a Win-Win for all parties to keep the relationships on track. If you are feeling underappreciated, though, I do have great bankers I can introduce you to. Your business matters to them, and you would be surprised how much they want you there.

The steps are simple if you decide to partner with us. First, a basic introduction or meeting (either on the phone or in-person). I simply want to learn about your business, if I can bring value, and how I can help.

Keep in mind that I do not choose everyone, just as not everyone will choose me. If I cannot help or we are not a match for each other, I will usually find someone to refer you to. There is NO charge for the initial meeting.

Chapter 32

Our Process

"Giant leaps are just a bunch of baby steps strung together."

Our Process

We have been fortunate to have our name out there through networking, some marketing, but mostly through people we know. Getting to work almost exclusively by referrals is a big blessing at 4 Kings Capital. The adage is true: Do a good job for someone, and you will be remembered. Of course, as a reader of our book, we would love to talk with you about your business to see if there is a way we can be a resource to you. Our general process outline is straight to the point, and we have included it below.

1. Receive an introduction from a referral source (or phone call).

Usually, we will receive an email introduction, or I will be given the name and phone number of the client that we are talking to. Other times someone will call saying So and So from such company told me I should talk to you. Great- we enjoy meeting new people.

2. Initial Phone call

When I get on the phone with a potential client, it can be casual, laid back or conversation, or all business. I leave this up to you and your level of comfort. I am simply trying to understand a few basic things:

A. What are you trying to accomplish? Tell me a little about your business. How long have you had it and so on? Are you buying a building, business, equipment, or refinancing, etc.
B. Second, where has this deal been before it got to me? This is an important bit of information for me personally because I get to see what feedback you received or even if we are dealing with contacts we might have in common. It helps move the process along, and my banker's brain starts going. I start to make mental notes evaluating where and who I can take the deal to.

    Although I offer consulting services to many clients who have no problem obtaining bank financing. A large portion of our business consists of deals that have been turned down somewhere, and we know this, so feel free to share this information with us. The quicker we know what we are dealing with, to faster we can get to an answer.
C. I ask questions to learn about your overall business and your character. This is done in basic conversation as we get to know each other. My head is already working as we talk. I size up if I think I can overcome the challenges of the credit.

Sometimes I find that the borrower has simply not found the right financing sources. Remember, your story may not have been told in a way that is clear to a lender, and that is okay. This entire thing is a learning process, and I help walk you through that. One of the things we pride ourselves on is our ability to tell your story in the way that the lender needs to hear it.

3. Initial Financial Review

If after we cover the initial conversation above and we see if I can provide value, our next step is for you to provide me financial information to review. There is no charge for this since it is part of how I screen clients.

I figure out quickly if we will be wasting each other's time. If the client cannot or will not provide this basic information to me to get a feel of the deal, we are done. The "Feel" is my banker brain that comes into play once the numbers are in front of me. That again is experience kicking in that shows me exactly what to look for.

Know this; I will not chase you to get me the basic information I need to size up the deal. I am busy too and have other clients needing my attention. If it takes you a while to get it to me, that is perfectly okay. My start time begins there.

I have had clients that wait months to get me the basic info and come with, "but we need to close like yesterday." No, you have been sitting on this for months and now want ME to hurry? It is not fair to anyone involved, including my lenders, my staff, our other clients, you, or myself. If I choose to put other things to the side to focus strictly on your deal, the negotiation on my price will be different.

I will get people calling and asking me to quote them rates and terms without providing me any information on their finances. That is not how this industry works. If this book is not proof of that, I do not know how else to explain that.

What they fail to see is any pricing I get (from my various lending sources) is going to be contingent on verifying the financial info. I have relationships with hundreds of lenders, and I am not going to waste their time or mine sending them some hypothetical situation to get pricing on a deal we have not even verified solid information on.

The true finance world does not work that way, contrary to what you see on TV or movies. The only way I can even begin to shop for the best deals is once I know what I am working with. Then I reassess my lending sources to know who works in that space. Unfortunately, not all lenders, banks, finance companies do the same kind of deals. Knowing different people in those spaces helps.

4. Fee Agreement and Structure

Once I have reviewed the initial package, I will usually have some questions to discuss with you, the borrower, to see if I think we can put something together. At that time, we will discuss the fee agreement structure. If I am hired to work the deals from start to finish or as a consultant, we can hammer out the details at this time.

Once we have come to an agreement, the client and I sign our engagement, and I go to market representing them.

A Quick Recap on what I Provide.

Basic Consulting agreement-

I give you advice, look over your financials, tell you how to put the packet together, but I am NOT driving the train. You talk to your banks, negotiate etc. Billing is either per project, per hour, or monthly retainer.

Consulting Plus Loan Packaging -

I give you advice, look over your financials, WE put the package together with you. You still find the lenders and negotiate it yourself. You drive the train. Billing depends on the complexity, size and urgency of the deal.

Complete Package Agreement

We handle everything. We give you advice on your company, go over financials, we package, search lending sources, and negotiate on your behalf keeping you up to date on the process. It is a one stop shop. Billing is usually up to a few points of the capital we find you.

Chapter 33

It is Your Dream; Make it Happen!

"When we strive to become better than we are, everything around us becomes better too." Paulo Coelho

The Wrap Up

Your Business is preparing for its transformation. Whether you work in the finance field or are a business owner, great changes are happening all around you. I want more than anything for you to be ready to tackle them head on. Some of you may be at a crossroads, while others are feeling defeated. I am here to remind you that people like you do not stay beaten or indecisive for long. You are careful but also the toughest group of risk-takers out there.

Now that you have some insight into what happens behind the scenes at a bank, I know you will be more confidant as you prepare your packages and talk to them about your business. As for my fellow bankers, I hope this will help as we receive stronger packages to make your jobs a little easier. May we be ready to open our minds on how to help these businesses.

I have already been asked what other things I can teach on finance, guidance for upcoming brokers, how to build relationships with people in the finance field (for networking), and even why I refused to stay the kid most people thought had no future. So, I have already started work on my next book. For me to do all the things I have in store, I can never stop learning. I hope you feel the same about what you do.

Never forget that you are more than just your title. Whether you work as a business owner, banker, CPA, broker, or any of the other finance fields, remember that you are adding to the ever-changing landscape of your communities. Your boldness to take charge is worth reaching those goals.

You are not just a restaurant that feeds people. You are where we go to celebrate or enjoy something new. It is a family taking a break from having to cook on long days. Some may just see a shop, but it is where someone goes to boost their self-esteem with a new outfit, lotion, or the million other things that make people happy.

Some of you may even offer the biggest service by aiding workers to provide for their families. There is a far bigger picture here. You are housing them, supplying entertainment, offering a service that makes their lives better- the lists go on and on. You are playing a role in improving people's way of life.

You were made for great things, and I am here to remind you that you are do not have to do it alone. My friends, if it is what you were called to do, then stop listening to the bull crap cynics. You have gotten this far, so do not stop now. You deserve to be there. You deserve to build those empires. Now get out there, kick some ass, and make it happen!

"Your dream was given to you. If someone else can't see it for you, that's fine; it wasn't given to them. It is your dream. Hold it. Nurture it. Cultivate it." Les Brown

About the Author

Bill King is the owner and Chief Commercial loan Consultant of 4 Kings Capital. Before starting his own business, he was in Banking for over 20 years receiving various awards, including The SBA Financial Services Champion (Oklahoma). He earned a Bachelor's in Business Management and is also a graduate of the SW Graduate School of Banking. He holds numerous licenses and certifications, including his CLFP, CLBB and is an Accredited Small Business Consultant (AASBC), speaker, and writer.

Made in the USA
Monee, IL
26 April 2023

32411277R00075